A COLE FAMILY IN AMERICA

(1633-2003)

A Cole Family in America

(1633-2003)

Descendants of Daniel Cole of
Plymouth Plantation (1633)

The
First Eleven Generations

David Charles Cole

To order additional copies of this book, contact:
Xlibris Corporation
1-888-795-4274
www.Xlibris.com
Orders@Xlibris.com
30408

CONTENTS

AUTHOR

DEDICATION

This short history is dedicated to the memory of members of the Cole family recorded in its pages. These individuals passed their DNA, talent, and strong Christian values on those who followed in the line.

Most of those named had been lost to history, unknown and unsung by subsequent generations. Only a few their names and none of the details of their lives were remembered. It seemed appropriate, therefore, to assemble in one place what names and details could be recovered through scores of hours scouring dusty library shelves and, in so doing, acknowledge the individuals whose genetic makeup and personal qualities continue to flow through this branch of the Cole family.

"Let us praise . . . our ancestors . . . Most left no memory, and disappeared as though they had not lived, perished as though they had never existed, they and their children after them. Yet, their offspring will continue forever and their glory will never be blotted out." (Ecclesiasticus 44:1-15)

PREFACE

What follows is a brief review of the ancestral line of one branch of a Cole family in America. It begins with Daniel Cole who traveled from England to the colonies in 1633 and ends with his descendant David Charles Cole in 2003. The span of the review covers 11 generations and 370 years.

I undertook this project to correct numerous inaccuracies found in Joseph A. Curtis' book, *The Descendants of Elisha Cole* (19) published in 1909, and to bring many additional historical details to light. It was also my desire to surface and record the contribution our forebearers made to the family and nation, being reminded that: "in death no one remembers you; or gives you thanks in the grave". (Psalm 6, vs. 5)

All that remains of the early years in the life of this branch of the Cole family is what can be gleaned from civil and church records, family Bibles and bits of oral history. Information on the lives of early members of the family is extremely limited. Their day-to-day struggle to satisfy immediate needs left them little time to contemplate a place in history or note any but major family events (i.e., births, baptisms, marriages, deaths). Precious little is known of the personalities of those who formed early Cole family units or the joys and pains they shared. I have attempted to fill this void by inserting relevant historical details. Still, we are left trying to view their world as through a pane of smoked glass, relying on our imagination to complete the picture.

Complicating my research is the fact that given names, particularly Daniel and Elisha, were used frequently in the branching of the family tree. At times there were three or four living family members named Daniel or Elisha, related as father, son, grandson, or cousin. This frequent occurrence required great diligence to sort out and ascribe relationships, events, activities, and possessions accurately.

Details on women in the family were most difficult to uncover, as they were not normally recorded. I have attempted to rectify this beginning in the ninth generation where information is more readily available. A more balanced reporting of the contribution of women in the family reflects the importance of the bloodline and heritage of each spouse.

I have included facts on the Cole surname, Cole family heraldry, and a few comments on the rigors and pitfalls of the genealogical research process. To assist the reader, I have incorporated a lineage summary tracing descendants from Daniel Cole to the present and several illustrations. Farm and home locations are noted when known to aid those wishing to visit the sites to come into closer contact with their physical roots.

Well-intentioned researchers who constructed histories without carefully referencing their sources confounded a search for genealogical details on the family line. Use of any such material must be made with great care. Information in this work is based on primary sources or publications quoting first-order sources. All sources are listed in the Bibliography and noted where appropriate throughout the text. Where I paraphrase, credit is given by noting the source following the text.

Our story in North America begins in 1633 when the names of three Cole brothers from Southwark, Surrey, England (John, Job, and Daniel) appear in the annals of the Plymouth Plantation. Daniel is indisputably our ancestor. As descendants of the union of his son, William Cole, and Hannah Snow of Plymouth, we are all descendants of <u>Mayflower</u> passenger Constance (Hopkins) Snow and her father Stephen Hopkins, a Pilgrim and signer of the Mayflower Compact.

All in this line who can trace roots back to Daniel and Ruth Cole of Plymouth are kinsmen with a common heritage. They can take pride in knowing that their ancestors were respectable, hardworking, stable, religious citizens in good standing in their respective communities:

> "*As a race, the Coles (descendents of Daniel Cole of Plymouth Colony) proved themselves sturdy, courageous, self-reliant and independent. They clung to the religious principles and hard-working habits of their Puritan ancestry, and throughout the length and breadth of America they have spread the example of the Gospel and the sturdier virtues which go to make the nation great.*"
> (19, p. 4)

The highest tribute to the dead is not grief, but gratitude. I hope that the information that follows will serve as a sustaining force for future family readers, providing an appreciation of their heritage and a feeling of historic stability in an increasingly inconstant world.

Introduction

Too often an easy indulgence presumes that family names borne by prominent or historic families in England assure some connection with the immigrant's family. In truth, most English emigrants to colonial New England and Virginia came from cottages, not manor houses. The few who were in any way related to nobility and gentry are well known, and have been since the time of their arrival.

A scion of an emigrant family would have had no cause to conceal his noble birth and allow his descendants to remain ignorant of their lofty heritage. Lords of the manor had little reason to leave England. They were particularly well situated at home, a condition they would not abandon readily. Instead, most early settlers had been tenants for generations and were eager to be landowners themselves.

Reliable investigations initiated on the basis of claims of noble birth have usually led to proof of yeoman origin. This is not to suggest that those who came were the driftwood of English life. On the contrary, these early pioneers were the backbone of English yeomanry. (7, pp. i-xiii)

Immigrants arriving between 1630-1640 (the period of the great migration) were born at the beginning of the 17ᵗʰ Century. They usually traveled with persons closely related by marriage or kinship. It is possible to get an idea of an emigrant's probable home area in England by knowing with whom he or she traveled, or the pastor connected with that group. Traveling groups usually located in the same town in the colonies. Likewise, former neighbors often secured adjoining land and continued old associations in the new country. It is through such relationships that the relocation of Daniel Cole from Southwark, Surrey, England, is documented.

The names of many immigrants who took part in the religious and economic exodus between 1630 and 1640 are found in official depositories scattered widely in England and America. These documents consist a few remaining lists of passengers permitted to travel to New England as certified by customs officials, principally of London, Ipswich, and Southampton. Unfortunately, existing lists are confined, with few exceptions, to the year 1635. The earliest list (March 1631/2) gives the names of only 16 adults and the name of the ship is omitted. Two others exist for the same year, but none for 1633, the year Daniel Cole arrived.

From 1606 to 1635 all emigrants were required by law to pledge allegiance to the Crown and "conformity to the principles of the Church of England," and their names were recorded in England. (55, p. 23) What became of the missing list, required by Order in Council, is a puzzle. This situation explains the difficulty in confirming the sailing date and the name of the ship on which the Cole brothers traveled from England.

One goal of my research was to establish a link between Daniel Cole of Plymouth (b. ca. 1614) and his family of origin in England. This proved a difficult task as records were poorly kept and many subsequently lost.

England had no official civil registration of births, marriages and deaths until 1837. For only three centuries prior to that (beginning 1538) the English church established a system of registering baptisms, marriages, and burials with records kept by each parish under an order of Thomas Cromwell, Lord Chancellor of the Realm. Records showing the existence of an individual were set down officially, not from birth, but the day of baptism. Unfortunately, the local clergy did not comply uniformly with this injunction. It took a second order 20 years later to make the registration effective.

In 1568, further provision for securing the safety of these parochial registrations was taken by church authorities ordering that copies of baptisms, marriages and burials be transmitted annually to the bishop of each diocese, where they were presumed to be carefully stored for reference. Instead, they became the prey of careless custodians who stored them in damp inaccessible places where they were either destroyed by vermin or decayed.

An added provision for security was made in 1597 when it was directed that existing registers written on paper should be transcribed into permanent parchment volumes. These provisions for securing the safety of the family records of the English people were adequate to accomplish the object of the Episcopate, but again the indifference of local clergy resulted in the loss and destruction of most of the earliest volumes. (6, pp. viii-xiii) For this reason, the English forebearers of Daniel Cole may never be known with certainty.

There is a similar problem in trying to identify the family name of Daniel's wife Ruth, distant mother to all those in this line. I devoted much time and effort trying to uncover her family name, and have set aside one section in this history to share what was learned. My hope is that what was uncovered will aid a later researcher similarly intent on finding out precisely who she was.

The work of the diligent researcher is only somewhat improved when searching the records of the Plymouth Plantation. The story of this planting of an English colony in the first half of the 17th Century becomes a study of its individual immigrants. It is an unfortunate that records needed to confirm important facts are often no longer available. In 1646, the Plymouth General Court ordered towns to appoint clerks to keep registers of marriages, births, and burials, as well as a record of divisions and purchases of land. In some towns, these ancient records were carefully preserved. Later, records for many communities on Cape Cod were stored in the Barnstable Courthouse. This safekeeping measure proved disastrous, for the courthouse was destroyed by fire October 22, 1827. Many valuable deeds and records were lost to posterity, greatly complicating the task of those researching early Eastham settlers such as Daniel Cole. (32, p. 17)

This paper relies on such documents as remain. I have tried to portray the lives of our ancestors with a high degree of accuracy and probability consistent with the rules of evidence. Primary documents, secondary sources, and reliable references to historic records were uncovered during hundreds of hours of rigorous research in libraries in Washington, Boston, New York, and elsewhere. They serve as the basis for the information found in this work relating to early members of the family.

A caution to future family researchers: The genealogical files of the Church of Jesus Christ of Latter-Day Saints (LDS) cannot always be relied upon to be completely accurate! Many "facts" on the early members of this Cole family in the LDS database were found by this author to be flat wrong, as proven by serious research and reference to first or second order documents. The Internet is rife with tempting details and speculative relationships that cannot be confirmed through rigorous research.

COLE FAMILIES IN ENGLAND— 200 TO 1633

This section is included for those who want to know something about early Cole families in England. As no connection has yet been confirmed between Daniel Cole and his ancestors, the information is of little interest from a geological standpoint. Those interested only in family details can jump ahead to the next section.

Much creative speculation has been expended on the origin and significance of the Cole family name. A analysis of ancient mythology by Jacob Bryant of Cypersham, an elaborate dissertation on the subject, notes Cole to be the same as Cou-el or Co-el. (4) Bryant says that Coel, the old Latin form of Coleus, meant a "sacred or heavenly person." Camden says that Cole is formed from the last syllables of Nicholas, and M.A. Lower in his *Essay on Nomenclature* says the same. It may also be a contraction of Agricola, "a tiller of the soil", as the name Cola occurs in the Doomsday Survey as the holder of much land in the counties of Hants, Devon, and Wilts during the reign of King Edward the Confessor.

Various spellings appear in official documents (e.g., Cole, Coles, Coal, Coale, Coel, etc.) but the name seems to have originated in Cornwall, Devon, and Somerset in southeast England. Whatever the origin, the name is recorded frequently in the early history of England beginning in the second century AD (16) The name appears 26 times in the Catalog of English Royal Family Lineage.

The traditional Cole coat of arms, depicted on the dust jacket of this book, are described as usually containing these symbols:

ARMS—Argent, a bull passant, gules (red), armed Or, within a bordure
    in Sable (black), bezantee;
CREST—A demi-dragon in vert (green);
MOTTO—"Deum Cole Regem Serva."

The motto translates: "Worship God, Save/Protect/Guard the King." With the noun "God", the Latin "colo" most always means, "worship". In this form of the command the word is identical to the name "Cole". In a clever play on words, the creator/writer of the motto wove the Anglican surname in the phrase as a legitimate Latin form.

The red bull is the heraldic symbol for strength and courage. Bezants (gold roundels) are symbolic of service against the Turks and denote Crusader ancestry. In armory the dragon is the symbol for the overthrow of a vicious enemy. The colors, according to heraldry signify: argent (silver) for sincerity; gules (red) for courage; and vert (green) for strength. (See back cover)

Heraldry is of ancient origin. It can be traced back to the Jewish tribes. A more elaborate form is found in the leading families of Greece and Rome who bore distinguishing symbols illustrative of or pertaining to deeds of valor or merit performed by their ancestors. In its modern sense, however, the heraldic art dates from the time of the Crusades and was reduced to its present system by the French. An erroneous idea is entertained by some that heraldic symbols denote an aristocratic or exclusive class. On the contrary, these badges of distinction were the reward of personal merit and could be secured by the humblest as well as the highest. They were more often testimonials and warrants of bravery, heroism, and meritorious deeds.

Without presuming any direct connection with the ancestors of Daniel Cole, it might benefit members of this family to hold a sense of the importance of the Cole name in English history. Most children have heard the ancient rhyme of "Old King Cole" that runs:

> "Old King Cole was a merry old soul,
> And a merry old soul was he.
> He called for his pipe and he called for his bowl,
> And he called for his fiddlers three."

The invasion by Julius Caesar in 55 B.C. heralded a Roman conquest and occupation that lasted until the 5th century A.D. The Old King Cole (Coel) made famous through this rhyme ascended to the throne about 238 AD. A hereditary King of Britain, he reigned over that portion of territory known today as Essex and Hertfordshire with his capital at Colnaecester, formerly the Roman City of Camulodunum and present town of Colchester. (4)

King Coel had the blood of many powerful tribes in his veins, among them the Saxons. The Roman Emperor sent troops to besiege the capital at Colnaecester in 293 A.D. King Coel withstood the city's containment for three years. The siege ended when he pledged the hand of his eldest daughter, Helena, to the Roman general Constantius Chlorus, who later succeeded him on the throne and was also briefly the emperor of Rome Constantius made his headquarters at Colnaecester. He and Helena traveled throughout the empire with their infant son, later Constantine the Great, born at Naissus. Constantine the Great, grandson of Old King Coel and the successor to his domain, was ultimately the ruler over the entire Roman Empire.

Some carriers of the Cole name are descendants of King Coel. Many were known to be of high antiquity and rank in Saxon times, as attested by the Doomsday Book and in the deed of King William the Conqueror given in 1070. The Cole name ranked among the half dozen families of prominence in England noted in the document. They are also recalled as peers in the time of Edward the Confessor.

Sir Richard Cole, Earl of the Isle of Wight in the time of Edward III, and various branches of the family possessed immense estates in Devon, Wiltshire, Cornwall, Somerset, Hampshire, and Lincolnshire. So prominent were they in the battles to preserve England in those days that they have retained crests and coats of arms, and many titles. (4, pp. 7-15)

Do we carry King Coel's genes or the noble blood of other luminaries in English history? Perhaps. However, it remains to be proven through further research. One family line in particular seemed worth pursuing based upon details uncovered in my research. It is presented here as an example of the frustration involved in trying to identify Daniel's father and family line.

The Earl of Buckingham, Thomas of Woodstock, acting for the King, knighted Sir John Cole, Knight of Nytheway in the Parish of Brixhano, in France before the Castle of Ardres on the 25th of July 1380. Sir John married Anne, the daughter and heiress of Nicholas Brodrugan, Knight. His son, Sir William Cole, Knight of Tamar, married Margaret, daughter of Henry Beaupell, Knight, and was the father of Sir John Cole, Knight, "who was in the Retynew of the Duke of Gloucester" and with Henry V at the Battle of Agincourt on Friday, October 15, 1415. He received his spurs for conduct on that field. He married Agnes, daughter of Sir Fitzwarine, Knight. They had four sons, John, Adam, William, and Robert. (4)

John Cole married Jane, the daughter of Robert Mergot of Devon. They had two sons, Simon and William Cole. William married Elizabeth, daughter of Sir Richard Weston of Wiltshire, Knight. Their son John married Mary, the daughter and heiress of Thomas Archdeacon of Devon. Their son, Thomas Cole of London, married Elizabeth, daughter of Thomas Hargrave of London. They had four sons (William, Thomas, Solomon, and Emanuel) and one daughter (Martha). (16, pp. 4-26)

Thomas Cole of London died in April 1571 and is buried in Allhallows Church, London. His son, William Cole, married Anne, daughter of Michael Colles of Bradwell, Bucks. Their son, William, born ca. 1588, married Elizabeth, daughter of Nathaniel Deads of London, a "silkman" (tradesman). (16, p. 27)

William Cole and Anne had seven sons: Arthur, William, Michael, Humphrey, Nathaniel, Thomas, "a man of much learning, much of a gentleman, and eminent for his piety and virtue," and Robert (Member of Parliament for Enniskillen). No date was uncovered for this marriage, but given William Cole's birth date (ca. 1588) it is unlikely any of his sons were born before 1608. That means their descendants would not have been of age to travel to Plymouth in 1633. A review of information available to this researcher also eliminated William Cole's brothers as possible links to Daniel, John, and Job. A dead-end.

There are other branches of the Cole family in the London area at the time worthy of future investigation. Roger Cole (son of William of Sudbury, son of William, second son of Sir John Cole, Knight) appeared on the register of St. Saviors Parish in Southwark in 1623, as do other Coles. Southwark was the home of Daniel Cole before he emigrated in 1633.

Alas, many tempting clues to Daniel's lineage in England exist but no family connections have been confirmed to date. What can be shown is that the brothers Daniel, John, and Job arrived in Plymouth from the London/Southwark area in 1633, leaving their mother, Frances, and at least two brothers Nathaniel and Zaccheus behind in England. The will of Frances' son Zaccheus is dated November 16, 1630, lists her and the five brothers, but does not name a male head of the household. (1, p. 119) It is reasonable to assume from this that Frances' husband and father to the boys was not with the family by that date. Whether dead, divorced or imprisoned, no record of him has been found. The register of wedding, christenings, and burials in the Parish of St. Olive in Southwark, considered to be the family parish, contains no entry that might lead to the identity of this family patriarch. There has been much speculation and careless attribution to fill the blankl and provide a name for Frances husband. Chasing these leads has consume much time and, in every instance to date, confirmed faulty research on the part of others.

At least one intriguing path remains to be followed. William Cole, Esq., of Gray's Inn, a bachelor, age 45, married Frances Appleton of Thundersley, Essex, age 44, widow of John Appleton, Esq., at St. Andrews, Holborn, May 16, 1609. (78) This date correlates with the estimated birth dates of the Cole brothers, whose mother's name we know was Frances. Additional research is needed to confirm or discount this connection.

Puritans, Pilgrims, and Planters

What circumstances led to the creation of the Plymouth Plantation? What caused the adventurers to leave England? What was the New World like when the Cole brothers arrived in 1633? Frances Stoddard's classic work *The Truth About the Pilgrims* is the source of the information that follows. (52)

An outstanding event in the birth of the United States was the arrival of the Mayflower with its small band of Pilgrims in 1620. Their descendants may be justly proud of being united by blood with this remarkable group of Christians.

The availability of the Bible in English beginning in the middle of the 16th Century convinced many Englishmen that the medieval Christian church had strayed too far from the practices and doctrines of Christ. Religious forms and beliefs, adopted from pagan religions or instituted by clerics to strengthen the political structure of the church, had replaced the simple teachings of Christ, and England had become largely controlled by an oppressive clergy holding vast sums of land. Fearless men and women, led by John Wickliffe and later reformers, laid the foundations of the Reformation that extended gradually across the countryside. Their inspiration came from a desire to return to the original faith. They were referred to as Protestants because they protested against the abuses of the existing church.

The history of England during the Middle Ages is largely an account of a chronic conflict between the state, composed of King and Parliament, and the church governed from Rome. Henry VIII did not lead the break with Rome that resulted in the Act of Supremacy in 1534. A great mass of the English people had long clamored for freedom from foreign clerical oppression. The King followed the desires of his subjects by allowing access to the New Testament translated into their native tongue by William Tyndale in 1525-26, and the Old Testament translated a few years later.

The boy king Edward VI succeeded Henry VIII in 1547. When Mary became Queen in 1553 she attempted to make England Roman Catholic again by force. She succeeded only in making England more Protestant before her death in 1558. The Anglican Church became firmly established under Queen Elizabeth I. It claimed its descent from the original Christian Church through the early English missionaries and denied that the papacy, created centuries after Christ's Crucifixion, had any right to control the church. (52, pp. 1-3) The formation of the Church of England and establishment of the Anglican tradition will become an important element in the life of the Cole family.

There was a split within the English Church under Elizabeth I that gave rise to the Puritan movement. The Puritans demanded a more thorough reformation to move the church closer to the original purity portrayed by the Scriptures. They did not intend to secede or separate from the English Church, but wished to work for reform from within its fold.

Puritanism first appeared as a protest against certain ceremonies and vestments required by law in the celebration of public worship, which the Puritans regarded as symbols of superstition. Many of the more educated in England joined the movement. They supported retaining the bishops, archbishops, and structure of the church, but wished to conform it to what they believed Christ would have desired. This did not go far enough to satisfy others who claimed that the church under the Apostles had been composed of gatherings of Christians who had no bishops or archbishops, whose leaders obtained authority from the congregation.

The term Pilgrim began to be used to identify the movement's members among the Mayflower passengers. (52, pp. 4-26) Strictly speaking, is should only be used in reference to the Separatists who originally left England for Leiden (Leyden), Holland, in 1620 with William Bradford. The term was Biblical in origin:

> *"These all died in faith, not having received the promises, but having seen them afar off, and were persuaded of them and embraced them, and confessed that they were strangers and pilgrims on the earth. For they that say such things declare plainly that they seek a country. And truly if they had been mindful of that country from whence they came out, they might have had opportunity to have returned. But, now they desire a better country: wherefore God is not ashamed to be called their God: for He hath prepared for them a city."* (Early translation, Hebrews, 11: 13-16)

From Maine on the extreme north to Virginia on the south, those who came to settle adopted the name "Planters" to distinguish themselves as those who came to fulfill a national obligation. The Pilgrim band had entered into a business arrangement with approximately 70 English venture capitalists (Merchant Adventurers) that agreed to pay for the trip, in return for which the settlers would engage in fishing, lumbering or whatever means would generate cash crops for transport and sale in England. (79) The places to which they came were called Plantations, and the Pilgrims referred to their new home as Plimmoth (sic.) Plantation—not Plymouth Colony. (6)

The communal cultivation of crops was practiced initially, with limited success. William Bradford, the colony's governor for nearly 36 years, wrote in his journal in 1623 that because of a corn shortage the colonists began to think how they could raise more. After much debate, they abandoned their doctrine of collective farming and assigned each family a parcel of land. All hands were thus made industrious, motivated by self-interest. The abandoning of collectivism unleashed energy through freedom, and marked the beginning of free enterprise farming in America,

This was the cultural environment Daniel entered when he arrived in 1633. Daniel was not a Pilgrim and may not have held Puritan beliefs, but he was a devout Christian seeking adventure and a better life. Through the marriage of his son William to Hannah Snow in 1686, subsequent generations in the line of William are descendants of the original Mayflower passengers.

DANIEL COLE— FROM ENGLAND TO PLYMOUTH

Family histories of various qualities have been written about the branches of the family descending from Daniel, Job, and John Cole. Until recently, none have attempted to trace the brothers back to England, detail how they journeyed to Plymouth, or confirm their connection with the <u>Mayflower</u> voyagers.

It is increasingly clear that the brothers traveled with merchant-adventurer William Collier (also spelled Colliar and Collyer) in 1633. Collier is variously described in historical writings as a brewer of London and as a grocer of Southwark, Surrey, across the Thames from London. Church records show William Collier lived in St. Mary Magdalen parish, Bermondsey, Surrey, before appearing on the records of St. Olave parish, Southwark, Surrey. It is in one or both locations that the Collier and Cole families first became entwined. (53, p. 268)

The borough of Southwark lay in Surrey south across London Bridge from London and was the largest town in the county at the time. Early histories refer to the region as St. Olave's Gate, Southwark. It rested at the foot of London Bridge and was an area filled with docks, warehouses, and businesses supplying London. It was also the habitat of wholesalers who, since they sold their wares in gross quantities, became known as "grossers." The Grocers Guild was large and powerful, and its members vied for many of the city's highest offices.

William Collier married Jane Clarke on May 16, 1611, at St. Olave parish, Southwark. His first wife, whose name is not recorded, most probably died at or immediately following the birth of their only child, Mary, who was baptized February 18, 1611/12, at St. Olave parish. Records there indicate William and his second wife Jane had 12 children, many of whom died in infancy. Their first son, John, died at age 2 in 1618. Other children, namely a second son to be named John, sons James, William, and daughters Catherine, Martha, Hannah, and Lydia, all died before age 10, five of them during the plague 1624-1625. Death at a young age was common at the time. The average life expectancy for the general population in London between 1604 and 1661 was 16 years.

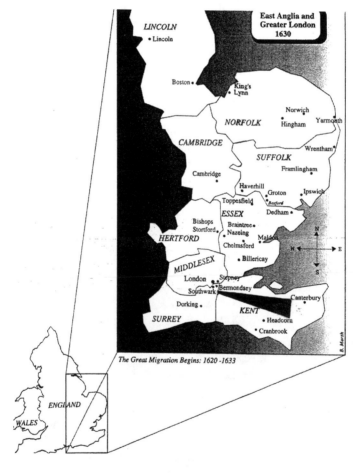

English Counties, 1630

William was a successful London merchant mentioned in Captain John Smith's 1624 General History of Virginia as one of the 70 "adventurers that raised Stock to begin and supply (reinforce) this Plantation . . . some gentlemen; some merchants; some handicraftsmen; some adventuring great sums and others small as their estates and affection served." Disasters, losses, and uncertainties made the investment risky. In November 1626, William Collier joined 41 others in an effort to recover part of their investment.

Despite his financial losses, William Collier's interest in the enterprise remained great, leading eventually to the decision to relocate his family to Plymouth in 1633. He was "a good benefactor of the Colony of New Plymouth before he came over, having been an Adventurer unto it at its beginning, and a very useful instrument of its jurisdiction after he arrived." (9, p. 158)

The Collier/Cole family connection surfaces in the will of Zaccheus Cole of St. Olave dated November 16, 1630. Zaccheus, "a citizen and grocer in London", appoints William Collier as overseer of his possessions, and Jean (sic) Collier witnessed the will. In it Zaccheus names his mother Frances and his brothers Nathaniel, John, and Daniel, and appoints his brother Job as executor. (1, p. 119) In the will on file in London, Zaccheus is spelled with only one "c". Most historians, including Stratton, use two. (53, p. 267)

Because of the ties with William Collier through wills and marriage, Southwark is most surely the region where Daniel, John, and Job worked and lived before immigrating to Plymouth. Stratton in his work *Plymouth Colony—Its History and People* places both the Cole and Collier families in St. Olave, Southwark, prior to 1633. (53, p. 267)

As noted, the name Collier appears frequently in the registry of St. Olave parish during the period 1611-1625. Of significance to the Cole line is the recorded baptism of Rebecca Collier on January 10, 1614/15. Rebecca was one of four surviving daughters by 1633 (Mary, Rebecca, Sarah, and Elizabeth). Rebecca married Daniel's brother Job on May 15, 1634, at Plymouth, on the same day Mary Collier wed Love Brewster, son of Elder William Brewster of the Mayflower. Both marriages are recorded in the St. Olave registry.

Job was likely born by 1610 based on the date of his marriage to Rebecca. He was literate and able to sign his name as witness to a deed. His brothers are assumed to have been equally educated and were likely younger, as Job was selected to be the executor of his brother Zaccheus' will, a responsibility normally bestowed on the eldest.

Job and Rebecca had at least two children: Rebecca, born August 26, 1654, in Eastham, and Daniel, date unknown. (53, p. 267) Rebecca may also have had a twin brother named Job and an older brother, John. (19,

p. 21) According to the historical sketch on William Collier by Kingsbury and Nickerson, Job's son Daniel married Mercy Fuller, daughter of Rev. Samuel Fuller of Middleboro. (29, p. 18) However, Curtis rightly notes that it was Daniel's son Daniel, Jr., who married Mercy Fuller, a fact confirmed by their still legible headstones in the Cove Burying Ground in Eastham. Job's son Daniel married Mercy Freeman, and Rebecca married Robert Nikerson.

Job was a constable at Roxbury and later at Nauset (Eastham), as well as a surveyor of the highways for that community. (53, p. 267) His date of death is still unknown, but he died before his wife Rebecca (Collier) Cole "widow of Job Cole" who died at about age 88 at Eastham, December 29, 1698. (53, p. 267)

The Collier/Cole family connection is confirmed again in the will of John Cole proved on January 7, 1637/1638. In it John refers to his brothers Job and Daniel, his sister-in-law Rebecca Collier (wife of Job), her sister Elizabeth, and Mr. Collier's men, Edward, Joseph, Arthur, Ralph, and John. (53, p. 268)

George Willison in his book, *Saints and Strangers*, notes William Collier arrived in 1633 accompanied by "three men, one woman and five children." (58, p. 486) The woman may have been his wife Jane and the children would have included his four daughters, already noted. There is no accounting for the fifth child, but passenger records at the time were notoriously inaccurate. The three men in the party were likely Mr. Collier's apprentices (not servants) Daniel, John, and Job Cole.

Historians Agnes and John Cooper confirm that William Collier "came to Plymouth on the ship Mary and James accompanied by four daughters and his apprentices, among them John, Job, and Daniel Cole." (18, pp. 64-65) According to this account, William's wife might not have accompanied them and "had probably died". This may be in error, as we know Collier's first wife had died and it is suspected that the "one woman" who traveled with him to Plymouth was his second wife, Jane. Reference to the voyage of the Cole brothers and the Collier family on the Mary and James is also found in Leon Clark Hills' Cape Cod Series, Vol. 1. (23) Unfortunately, neither author identifies a source document. Peter Coldham's *The Compete Book of Emigrants—1607-1660* confirms a ship of that name was bringing passengers to Plymouth during the period, but does not contain complete passenger lists. (13)

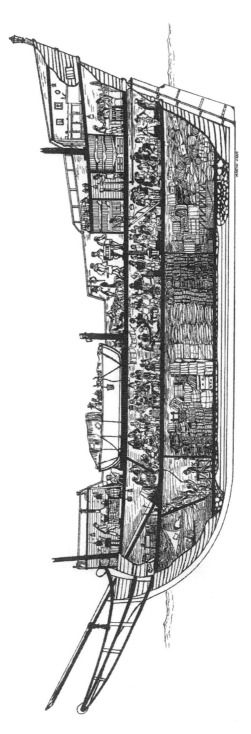

The Mary and James, 1633

While no official record giving precise dates for the 1633 passage has been found, it is certain that the brothers arrived before September 14, 1633, as the will of Richard Langfield, who died on that date in Plymouth, notes a debt owed to Job Cole. (53, p. 267) It is also now certain that the Coles were apprentices in the grocery or an associated trade and traveled to Plymouth from Southwark together in the company of William Collier and his family.

Daniel's birth year is estimated to have been 1614, based on his age of 80 at the time of his death in December 1694. This would have made him age 18 or 19 at the time of his arrival in the colonies and 29 when he married.

STEPHEN AND CONSTANCE HOPKINS— THE MAYFLOWER CONNECTION

Stephen Hopkins was born in England ca. 1582. He arrived on the Mayflower on November 11, 1620, accompanied by his second wife Elizabeth (Fisher), whom he married in St. Mary's Church, Whitechapel, London, on February 19, 1617/8. His first wife Mary (family name unknown) died May 9, 1613, and is buried at Hursley in Hampshire, England.

His new wife traveled with him on the Mayflower, along with his son Giles (Gyles) born by his first wife in England ca. 1608; his daughter Constance (Constanta) also by his first wife, born in London in 1606; Damaris, a daughter by his marriage to Elizabeth, born in England ca. 1618, and Oceanus, born to Elizabeth at sea; plus his two menservants. (5) He was not a Pilgrim, but one of the "Londoners" or "strangers" on the Mayflower, an adventurer recruited for the voyage.

Stephen is considered to have been the son of Stephen Hopkins, Sr., a clothier in London. He served as clerk to the chaplain on the vessel Sea Venture that sailed from London on June 2, 1609, bound for Virginia, part of a fleet of nine bringing supplies and reinforcements to the Jamestown settlers. The ships sustained damage during a hurricane and the company of 150 from the Sea Venture washed ashore in Bermuda on 28 July. Two ships were built from wood salvaged from the Sea Venture, and the party proceeded to Virginia, arriving in

Jamestown on May 24, 1610. No evidence is found of his residence there, and it is presumed he returned to his home just outside the London Wall in 1611 or 1612. He returned to the colonies on the Mayflower in 1620.

His daughter Constance who traveled with him married Nicholas Snow from Hoxton, Middlesex, England, on or before May 22, 1627, at Plymouth. By 1644, many families had determined to leave Plymouth and settle in Nauset (Eastham), on Cape Cod. Nicholas Snow, Constance (Hopkins) and their sons and daughters were among this number. Their daughter Ruth, born ca. 1644, married John Cole, first-born of Daniel and Ruth Cole, on December 12, 1666, at Eastham. Followers in this Cole line are Mayflower descendants. (5, p. 20)

Daniel and Ruth's son Israel married widow Mary (Paine) Rogers, April 24, 1679, a granddaughter of Nicholas and Constance (Hopkins) Snow. Israel is said to have been the wealthiest man in New England at the time of his death. Followers in this Cole line are Mayflower descendants. (5, p. 37)

Constance's brother Giles married Catherine, daughter of Gabriel Whelden of Yarmouth, Cape Cod, on October 9, 1639. Their son Joshua married Mary, daughter of Daniel and Ruth Cole, on May 26, 1681, forming a third marital connection between the Cole and Hopkins families. (5, pp. 9-10). Followers in this Cole line are Mayflower descendants. (5, p. 26)

Of greatest consequence to this work is the birth of Stephen Snow, son of Constance and Nicholas Snow, born ca. 1636. He married the widow Susanna (Deane) Rogers on October 28, 1663, at Eastham. Their daughter Hannah Snow (granddaughter to Constance Hopkins and great-granddaughter to Stephen Hopkins) was born there January 2, 1666. She married Daniel and Ruth's son William on December 2, 1686, marking the fourth familial connection with Daniel Cole's offspring and Stephen Hopkins. It is through this marriage that members of the Daniel Cole family in the line of William are descendants of two original Mayflower voyagers and a signer of the Mayflower Compact that established the first fully representative form of government in North America. (5, p.58) (46, pp. 20, 100-101)

Daniel and Ruth Cole's son Daniel established a fifth family Mayflower connection when he married Mercy Fuller, daughter of Rev. Samuel and Elizabeth (Brown) Fuller, date unknown. Mercy was a granddaughter of Samuel Fuller who accompanied his father, Edward, on the 1620 Pilgrim voyage. Samuel Fuller was a deacon of the church in Leiden and later in Plymouth, and one of the forty-one signers of the Mayflower Compact.

EARLY MIGRATION TO CAPE COD

The Pilgrims' destination at the time of sailing was the northern Virginia Territory roughly in a region where New York City is today. Separatists were enlisted to fill out the required number for the voyage. Those additional passengers are many times referred to as the "strangers," since they were not all Separatists. All of the passengers who came on the Mayflower in 1620 became known as Pilgrims, whether they were Leiden Separatists (sometimes referred to as the "saints") or "sinners".

The second ship, the Speedwell, proved unseaworthy, and the Mayflower was forced to make the voyage to America alone. Many of the Leiden members decided that they did not wish to make the voyage and returned to Holland. The Mayflower made her final departure from Plymouth, England, on September 16, 1620.

She was one of the larger merchant vessels of her day. A worthy sailer, the Mayflower made the crossing in 66 days at about 2 miles per hour against the strong currents of the Gulf Stream and stormy winds of the North.

The Pilgrims were undoubtedly aware of the dangers they would face in the North Atlantic at that time of year, but decided to begin the voyage anyway. Their money was at an end and English authorities were still searching for William Brewster, who was concealed on the ship. Fortunately, Master Christopher Jones, the skipper, had sailed the waters of the North Sea during stormy seasons, and knew how to handle Mayflower under such stress.

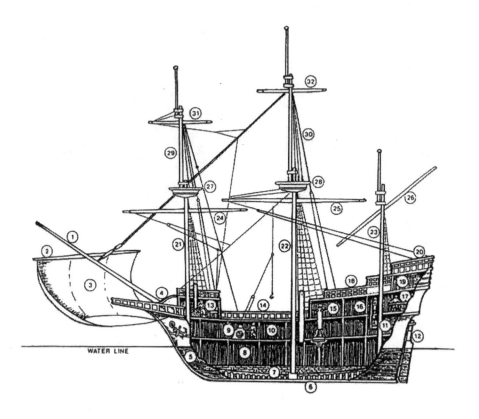

MAYFLOWER

1.	BOWSPRIT.	17.	GREAT CABIN.
2.	BOWSPRIT YARD.	18.	QUARTER DECK.
3.	SPRITSAIL.	19.	CHART HOUSE.
4.	BEAKHEAD.	20.	POOP DECK.
5.	HULL.	21.	FOREMAST.
6.	KEEL.	22.	MAINMAST.
7.	BALLAST.	23.	MIZZEN MAST.
8.	MAIN HOLD.	24.	FOREYARD.
9.	ANCHOR WINDLASS.	25.	MAIN YARD.
10.	THE 'TWEEN DECK.	26.	MIZZEN YARD.
11.	TILLER FLAT.	27.	FORE TOP.
12.	RUDDER.	28.	MAIN TOP.
13.	FORECASTLE (FO'C'SLE).	29.	FORE-TOPMAST.
14.	MAIN DECK.	30.	MAIN-TOPMAST.
15.	CAPSTAN.	31.	FORE-TOPSAIL YARD.
16.	STEERAGE (WHIPSTAFF).	32.	MAIN-TOPSAIL YARD.

The <u>Mayflower</u>, 1620

The initial heading would have taken them to the mouth of the Hudson River, but the northerly Gulf Stream caused the ship to drift north. According to William Bradford's account on November 9, 1620, the passengers finally spied land that "we deemed to be Cape Cod, and so afterward it proved."

The Mayflower continued its journey south around the cape, but the early winter winds forced the crew to turn back. Bradford wrote: "We put around again for the Bay of Cape Cod: and returned upon the 11 of November, where we came to an anchor" in the area at the tip of the cape. By December 11, with winter hard at hand, the voyagers decided to stay and explore Plymouth Harbor, named several years earlier by Captain John Smith. They soon elected to winter in the area of a Wampanoag village that had been deserted when disease killed many native Indians. (53, p. 20)

It had been a difficult 66-day journey in rough late-season seas. One hundred and two passengers sailed from England, 34 of them children. One passenger died enroute, four at Provincetown Harbor; one was born at sea (Oceanus Hopkins) and one in Provincetown Harbor. Thus, 99 arrived in Plymouth Harbor. Only 52 were still alive when the next ship, Fortune, arrived in November 1621. Most died during the winter of 1620/21. Of the 34 children, ten had died before spring. Many adults died of infection or from a lack of adequate food. Only five of the original 18 married women survived to cook and care for the sick. (79)

In the fall, before the arrival of the Fortune, the small band of survivors celebrated what is traditionally considered to be the first Thanksgiving. The three-day harvest festival of food and athletic games was shared with local Indians who had taught the pioneers how to grow native crops and contributed five deer to the feast. No new settlers arrived until July 1623, but fishing ships and others engaged in the colonizing venture anchored in the harbor occasionally.

However much they wanted to escape England and its "corruptions", they tried to kept faith with their English ways—ways of talking, dressing, thinking, eating, and drinking. Being separated from England gave them a religious freedom, but the cost was cultural isolation and an extremely harsh life. Discouraged and afraid, many early colonists simply gave up and left. As many as one in six chose to return home to England during the 1630s and 1640s. (79)

Those who remained from the Mayflower settled at Plymouth, finding nearby Cape Cod both a blessing and a nuisance. It was a blessing as a granary from which friendly Indians supplied them with corn. It was a nuisance geographically because it extended the over water route to New York where Plymouth settlers traded with the Dutch. The voyage around the cape was long and dangerous.

Explorers looking for corn on the cape soon discovered that the combination of the Scusset Creek and Manomet River cut the cape nearly in two at one point on the south. This realization spawned the idea of avoiding the sea passage around the cape by using these streams and a short carry overland from one to the other. By 1627, settlers were employing this channel as an established trade route and erected a safehouse near the headwaters of the Manomet River. They kept two men there and built a shallop large enough to navigate the waters of Nantucket Sound. This new passage was so successful that within a few years Plymouth was trading actively with the Connecticut River area and New York. The colonists ceased to think of the cape as a hindrance and, by degrees, began to realize that it was also a good place to live. The area was annexed to the territory of the Plymouth Colony in 1630, which soon gave rise to several new settlements. (30, p. 52)

Barnstable County Townships, 1685

The first of the new communities on Cape Cod were Sandwich, Barnstable, Yarmouth, and Nauset (also Nawsett, Nosett) later known as Eastham. When the scattered communities composing the Plymouth Colony developed a legislative form of government, these communities joined the association and sent deputies to the colonial legislature. The colony court sent out joint expeditions against the Indians in 1642 and again in 1645, as the dreaded Narragansetts were causing much uneasiness by "their unfriendly attitude".

Nauset, the last of the original four cape towns to be founded, was settled by a solidly united group of church members. It was endowed at birth with a richer strain of Pilgrim blood than Sandwich, Yarmouth, or Barnstable, as the settlers came largely from the Massachusetts Bay Colony community of Scituate and the Plymouth Plantation.

By 1640, Plymouth had begun to suffer from the loss of a handful of her citizens here and a handful there as they emigrated to one or another of the many new settlements quickly springing up throughout the area. Business in the old town was not what it had been. Men began to grumble and for want of a better grievance declared that the trouble was poor soil. They decided to move in a body—to transplant the entire population—leaving Plymouth as the Indians had left it before.

Governor William Bradford had reserved three tracts of land on the cape, one of which was Nauset, for the use of the original purchasers and the "Old Comers". The soil there was purported to be the best in the Colony. This fact induced the authorities to send a small party to the cape to look at the property. They returned with the discouraging verdict that there was room there for only a portion of the population of Plymouth. In April 1644, the more vigorous among the Plymouth population departed for the area. Freemen relocating there included John Doane, Edward Bangs, Nicholas Snow, John Smalley, and Joseph Rogers. (41, p. 76) There were 49 in the original group. Daniel Cole was among the earliest settlers to move onto the cape.

The pioneers from Plymouth arrived in time to plant corn and beans, and had the spring before them to build their houses. The soil met their expectations and they were happy in the new location. Successive crops of wheat, corn, and other grains were produced, furnishing a large amount for export. Several fresh-water ponds dotted the surface and the soil was alluvial.

For several years the crops were good and the town prospered. The land had been "legally purchased" from the Indians, as it had been in the earlier cape towns. It is hard to take such transactions seriously, however, or to see anything but the mere letter of truth in Governor Winslow's boast "the English do not possess one foot of land in the Colony but was fairly obtained by honest purchase from the Indian proprietors", when they commonly gave no more than a hatchet for a square mile of land.

Church members had settled the original colony and religious bodies continued to institute the law and government. No one could be a Freeman and take part in the affairs of the church or the body politic unless he (men only) was a member and, under this rule, the church even gave or refused the right to settle.

The concept of "Freemen" went back centuries in England as a means to describe those who were not serfs, but enjoyed the freedom of a town. In Plymouth the right to vote was restricted to Freemen elected to this privilege by the General Court. Few who traveled to the colonies before 1630 were Freemen. In October of that year more than 100 Massachusetts Bay Company colonists demanded Freeman status that would give them the right to vote and to be involved in the affairs of local government. These and a few others were made Freemen in 1631. (53, pp. 147-149)

Prior to the spring of 1635, the general court promulgated no penal laws. The moral laws of Moses and the New Testament governed the people. In 1636, legislative powers where formally vested in the full body of Freeman who were given sole lawmaking powers. They served as the legislature and elected the Governor.

Six of the original settlers of the area, including Nicholas Snow, erected their first dwellings in the south limits of the present town of Eastham. Others who joined them from Plymouth included the families of Daniel Cole, Job Cole, Mark Snow, and Stephen Hopkins. (20, pp. 722-723) How much of a community the town had become by 1643 is gathered from records listing Freemen and those capable of bearing arms. Daniel and Job were among the 16 Freemen of the town and the 52 allowed to bear arms. (20, p. 460)

When the settlement was completed its second year, Old Colony officials saw it had prospered and consented to its being incorporated as a township on June 2, 1646. Five years later, on June 7, 1651, the name changed from Nauset to Eastham. (30, pp. 58-60)

Before county courthouses were established, various towns were permitted to hold "Select Court". So many were the rules regulating the conduct of the public the general court couldn't admonish punishment of all the petty offenses, of which there were many: three hours in the stocks and a fine of five shillings was imposed for swearing; two hours in the stocks and five shillings for drunkenness; fines varying from shillings to pounds for lying; and public whippings at "carts tail" for "whoredom", acts of fornication, or the birth of a bastard child. Whipping while tied at the tail of a cart as it was being drawn through a town was considered a more harsh punishment than public whippings at the town post.

"Selectmen" were elected in Eastham starting in 1663. Daniel Cole was elected a selectman in Eastham for nine years beginning in 1667. For many years the court at Plymouth ruled even these offices with religious severity, causing them to whip all who denied orthodoxy and place in the stocks those who stood outside the meetinghouse during service.

The population of the towns of Plymouth Colony increased rapidly and it became necessary to divide the colony into counties in 1685. Cape Cod towns formed Barnstable County with Barnstable as the shire. A courthouse was erected there in 1689. (32, p. 18)

DANIEL AND RUTH ON CAPE COD

Daniel and his brothers were not the first Coles in the Colony. James Cole, not related to Daniel, built the first house on the bluff overlooking "the rock" ca. 1633. It came to be known as Cole's Hill. His son James, a "vintner", kept a tavern and inn there from 1638 to 1660 in a house originally built by Governor Winslow, the oldest structure in Plymouth at the time. (53, p.213)

Daniel arrived in Plymouth (1633), lived in Duxbury (1640), Marshfield (1642), and Yarmouth before settling in on Cape Cod in ca. 1644. He was joined by Ruth, whom he married ca. 1643. Based on their birthdates (ca. 1614 and ca. 1627) he was 29 and she 16 when they married.

Daniel's brother Job relocated from Duxbury to Nauset in 1639 with his wife Rebecca (Collier) and four children. Daniel and Ruth followed. Members of this Cole family line lived on Cape Cod for more than a century before moving west in search of more land and a better life.

As noted, the connection with William Collier suggests Daniel might have been a grocer's apprentice when he traveled to Plymouth Plantation. However, Pope in his *Pioneers of Massachusetts,* describes Daniel Cole as a "tailor in Yarmouth" in 1643, having "accounts with Thomas Hawkins for Mr. Pollington of London". (42, p. 109)

Whatever his original trade, Daniel soon owned land in the colony. He was granted 50 acres near Yarmouth on April 6, 1640, but was likely not involved in farming that land and soon sold it. Deeds are recorded for other land he sold in Duxbury in 1649 and "fifty acres and meadow in Marshfield" sold in 1650. (15, pp. 67-68)

Daniel became a worker of the soil after relocating to the cape and was prominent in municipal affairs, active in civic life, and contributor to the administration of local governments. He was an "able-body man" in Yarmouth in 1643; is listed along with Job as able to bear arms "to provide for defence against assault" that same year; was proposed for Freeman status in June 1644 and admitted/sworn in June 4, 1645; and on the jury that convicted Alice Bishop for infanticide on August 1, 1648. (15, p. 67) Alice confessed to murdering her daughter, Martha Clarke, the daughter of her first husband. She stated she regretted the act, but was sentenced by the jury to be hung for her actions.

He was Town Clerk in Eastham in 1652 and served as Deputy for Eastham to the Colonial Court at Plymouth for a total of 12 years beginning in 1654. His name appears on a list of legal voters in 1655 along with Job Cole, Giles Hopkins, John Smalley, Mark and Nicholas Snow, and 23 other citizens. He was Constable in 1664 and Selectman for nine years beginning 1667. He also served as a member of the Yarmouth County Band (a form of militia) in 1664. (19)

On June 10, 1661, Daniel was licensed to retail, draw, and sell "strong waters and wine" in Eastham "provided that he always be furnished with good wine for the supply of those in need among them." The early settlers were very careful to control the sale of liquor in order to limit its abuse and availability to local Indians. Only individuals of high moral character were entrusted to engage in the drawing and selling of "strong waters" and wine. (74)

Daniel was appointed Inspector of Shot and Leade in 1662: "Every Township shall provide a barrel of powder and lead bullets answerable to be kept by some trusty men in every town that it may be ready for defence in tyme of needed and danger." (15, p. 67) (74) In 1668 he, along with Thomas Hinckley, Nathaniel Bacon, Constant Southworth, John Allen, John Chipman, and Lieut. Morton, was appointed by the Old Colony Court to purchase for Gov. Prence the place at Plain Dealing in Plymouth that had been selected for the residence of the governor. (74)

Daniel was also appointed by the town to use his "best endeavors to put forward or encourage the Indians" to kill wolves, which at this time and more than 30 years afterward were numerous and troublesome within the precinct. (74)

The original Cole farm located in Eastham was adjacent to Cape Cod Bay, just north of the point where a party of Pilgrims first encountered Nauset Indians while scouting by boat on December 8, 1620. The location of the farm is established clearly in local records. Today a portion of the land is in a Town of Eastham conservation area known as Wiley Park and Green, immediately north of the eastern terminus of Cole Road and bounded by Great Pond on the east and Bridge Pond to the south.

Alice Lowe's *Nauset on Cape Cod, A History of Eastham* published by the Eastham Historical Society and paraphrased below describes life in the area during the time Daniel and his sons cleared the land, farmed, and raised their families. (32)

It was a life of few possessions and much hard work. Initially homes were practical and of rude construction with outside walls of hand-hewn vertical planks, roofs thatched with marshland grasses common to the area, and a few windows made of oiled paper. They were sparsely furnished with daily necessities: handmade tables, chairs, and beds, wooden plates, a few large pewter serving platters or porringers (handled bowls in which stews called portages were eaten), an iron kettle or two for cooking over the fire, candle sticks, an hourglass, and a Bible and Psalm Book.

Notwithstanding the hardships and privations of the first settlers, they had much to encourage them. The surrounding oaks furnished lumber. Cape Cod Bay was abundant with fish and the forest rich with game.

Soon, frame houses were built to replace the early crude homes. The newer homes were usually built facing south, despite the direction of the road they were built near, to afford the greatest amount of heat from the sun. Many were two stories in front with the roof sloping down to one story in the rear. Others were square one-story structures with deeply pitched roofs. The styles became knows as the "salt box" and the "Cape Cod."

Each had a large central fireplace and chimney before which normally stood the flax and spinning wheels, a large handloom, and the ubiquitous cradle. There wives did the spinning and weaving, dyeing, fashioned family clothing, made soap, dipped bayberry candles, and cooked meals in iron kettles that swung over the fire. They also braided colorful rugs and hemmed curtains of thin homespun to filter the sunshine streaming through the windows. Their daily tasks were arduous and many women died while very young or were left alone when dangers and difficulties of pioneering took the lives of their husbands. Because the hardships of the new life demanded companionship and aid, remarriages were common following the death of a spouse.

Men in the community shared the work of managing a farm while helping each other clear fields and build homes. There was a communal pasture and each man was given an "ear-mark" with which to brand his stock. Few had sheep and cattle in the early years, but they were commonly owned before the turn of the century. Soon, each family had a large barn for sheltering animals and storing the harvest.

The Pilgrims had learned the value of windmills during their years of refuge in Holland. Almost every Cape Cod barn bore a picturesque water-pumping mill that filled storage tanks above the wells. A few farms even had larger mills to grind grain. The settlers raised large crops of corn, wheat, rye, and flax. Corn was the principal product. Wolves, mockingbirds, and crows remained a menace to the town and harvests.

History often confuses the religious practices of the Pilgrims and Puritans. The Pilgrims and most who settled with them were Congregationalists, not

Puritans. They practiced no tortures of self-denial, but exercised tremendous discipline within the community. They liked to laugh, dance, sing, and wear bright colors.

A Congregational Society, the first in Eastham, was transferred from Plymouth in 1644 and a meetinghouse was soon erected on the hill north of Town Cove. A burial ground was nearby. The meetinghouse was a simple structure about 20 feet square with a thatched roof and openings on the sides for use in firing muskets in defense against the Indians, had it become necessary. The parishioners were very conservative with many laws that confirmed their determination to maintain a religious community. In 1651 the General Court ordered, "if any lazy, slothful or profane persons in any of the towns neglect to attend public worship, they shall pay for each offense ten shillings or be publicly whipped." (74)

As in England, the churchyard was also as a burial ground. The old Cove Burying Ground next to the site of the original meetinghouse remains to this day and holds the graves of many Eastham settlers. Regrettably, few grave markers are still in place, as many were originally made of wood. Even the inscriptions on some of the stone markers are so worn by the elements they are no longer legible. Headstones for Daniel and Ruth's son Daniel and his wife Mercy can still be found here. They are adjacent to a commemorative marker over the burial spot of <u>Mayflower</u> traveler Constance Hopkins, the grandmother to William Cole's wife Hannah Snow. Her brother Giles is buried nearby.

Given that participation in the church community was required, several Cole family members are buried in the Cove Burying Ground. The site is only two miles from the original Cole farm. Coles in the line at the time were true to the faith and likely worshiped regularly at the original Congregational church. This is probably the spot where Daniel (d. 1694), his wife Ruth (d. 1694), their son William (d. ca. 1737), and his wife Hannah (d. 1737), and others in the line are buried. This is not a certainty, as Daniel and Ruth might have resided in nearby Truro and/or Wellfleet at onetime and later owned land in Harwich that he willed to his first born, John. (74) The expanse of the Cove Burying Ground serves as evidence that many of the earliest markers are now gone. No complete record remains to establish the names of all who rest there.

No mention of a school is found in the records of Eastham until 1666, when Jonathan Sparrow was hired to teach reading, spelling, writing and arithmetic. Up to that point, all children were "home taught".

Daniel lived with his family in Eastham until he died there on December 21, 1694, at age 80, just six days after Ruth died on December 15th at age 67. He died intestate. This seems unusual for a man of his standing in the community and of quite considerable means. This lack of a will, coupled to the near simultaneous death of both Daniel and Ruth in December 1694, may indicate some general sickness in Eastham that winter that took them with little warning or preparation.

Barnstable County Probate Records detail the distribution of Daniel and Ruth's assets among their 11 adult children, based on an inventory completed on December 24, 1694. The settlement was witnessed by all the children on January 15, 1694/95. Interestingly, sons Israel, William, and Daniel witnessed by signature. All others did so "by a mark", indicating perhaps only those three were literate.

Daniel and Ruth raised their family in the rustic environment, as did others in the direct line, including their son William and his wife Hannah Snow whom he married there December 2, 1686. William and Hannah's son Elisha, next in the line, was born in Eastham on January 26, 1688/89 and married Anne (last name unknown) there ca. 1711. Their son Elisha, Jr. was born in Eastham in 1719 and married there (1) Priscilla Smalee (sic) on December 13, 1739. After her death he married (2) Hannah Smalley who, despite the inconsistent spelling of the family name, was likely Priscilla's cousin.

Members of the Cole family lived and farmed on Cape Cod for 103 years beginning in 1644. Four successive families in the line made the cape their home. Elisha, Jr., was the last in the line to live on Cape Cod. He and Hannah remained in the area until 1746 when they relocated with their three sons to Dutchess County (now Putnam County) New York, most likely beginning the journey from the port at Harwich and sailing up the Connecticut or Housatonic River. From there they would have traveled overland through the Taconic Mountains, finally settling not far from the present town of Carmel, New York. They may have lived in or near Harwich for a time before sailing, as Daniel had owned land there.

The connection with Cape Cod ended with Elisha and Hannah relocated to Dutchess County to begin a new life in what was then wilderness. Brothers, sisters, and cousins remained behind, however, and the Cole family name is found up and down the length of the cape today.

RUTH—MYSTERIOUS MATRIARCH

It is sad to report that there is considerable disagreement in genealogical writings about Ruth's maiden name, and no record has been found of her birth or her marriage to Daniel ca. 1643. She would devote more than 50 years to her marriage, toiling next to her husband and raising 11 children under harsh conditions. Five of her children would marry <u>Mayflower</u> descendants forming direct lines with the earliest Plymouth settlers. Yet, nearly nothing is known about her with certainty and her family name has not been clearly established.

In a deed dated October 15, 1659, William Collier refers to Daniel as his "son-in-law." This has led some to believe incorrectly that Ruth was a daughter of William Collier. Neither his home parish nor Plymouth Colony records show William ever had a daughter named Ruth.

At the time the term "son-in-law" meant "son by law and not by nature." It was used in referring, not only to a daughter's husband, but also a stepson and sometimes to other close male relatives. William Collier brought Daniel with him to Plymouth as his apprentice in 1633. At that time Daniel was not yet of legal age and his father was deceased. Collier may have been his legal guardian, leading to the reference as "son-in-law". Job Cole married Collier's daughter Rebecca, making Daniel Cole her brother-in-law. Any of these connections might have prompted William Collier to refer to Daniel Cole as his "son-in-law."

It is more likely that William Collier was referring to Job and Rebecca's son Daniel. Supporting this proposition is the fact that William Collier died after May 29, 1670. The exact date unknown. On October 29, 1671, the court ordered that Daniel Cole, son of Job and Rebecca, be given items from the estate as specified on a paper given to him by Mr. Collier. (53, p. 267-268)

In their history of the Thomas Cooper family, Agnes and John Cooper assert she was probably Ruth Chandler, daughter to Edmond and Elizabeth (family name unknown) Chandler (Chaundeler) of Duxbury. (18, p. 64) Edmond's family has Mayflower connections to John Alden. (60) Daniel had owned land and lived in Duxbury three years before he married and would likely have known the Chandler family. The Coopers also note the marriage of Mary (Paine) Rogers to Israel Cole and refers to him as the son of "Daniel and Ruth (Chandler) Cole of Eastham". (18, p. 64) That would seem to confirm the Cole/Chandler family relationship, but it is not correct.

Edmond was born in London, probably ca. 1588/9, the son of John and Jane (Gitton) Chaundeler (sic). He married and moved his family to Barbados ca. 1625/26 and arrived in Plymouth in 1632/33 where he settled in Duxbury (originally spelled Ducksborough). (33) His will dated May 3, 1662, mentions a daughter Ruth. (33, p. 11) No date for her birth can be established in Chandler genealogical records, and no age is ascribed in the will. She is, however, listed as the last of his seven children and born after his son John in 1638. If correct, she could not have been Daniel's wife as she would have been less than five years of age when Daniel married ca. 1643. Also, Edmond Chandler's will of 1662 refers to her as "Ruth Chaundeler" not Ruth Cole. Daniel and his Ruth had been married for 18+ years by 1662 and her legal name was Ruth Cole.

The *Mayflower Society's Silver Books Volume 2* and *15* (47 and 48, p. 163) confirm that widow Mary (Paine) Rogers married Daniel and Ruth's son Israel in Eastham on April 24, 1679, and refer to Israel as "a descendant of Pilgrim Stephen Hopkins." This could only be if Ruth were related to Stephen Hopkins, because we know Daniel was not. The Hopkins line has been researched extensively without surfacing anyone in the family named Ruth with a birth date suitable for marriage to Daniel ca. 1643.

John D. Austin's masterwork *Mayflower Families Through Five Generations Volume 6—Steven Hopkins (Second Edition)* lists Israel and William Cole as the "son of Daniel and Ruth (___) Cole" indicating that her family name and lineage are unknown. The Third Edition published six years later, however, states in four instances that Ruth's family name was "Chester" (5, pp.20, 26, 37, 58), yet this is not confirmed as fact in any of the sources referenced quoted by the author.

While Curtis, Austin, and others have come to accept that Daniel's wife was Ruth Chester, no original document has been found referring to her as Ruth Chester before her marriage and the name does not appear in any of the records of Plymouth Colony.

The cause of much of the confusion and the convention of ascribing her to the Chester family is Gustave Paine's work *"Daniel Cole and Ruth Chester"*. (39)

It is a poorly referenced series of notes, not carefully researched. Regrettably, Austin and others now use it as a source without confirming Paine's claim of a Chester family connection. Other researchers who respect Austin and his work have now begun to accept "Ruth Chester." It is a careless and undocumented conclusion.

As stated, no one by that name is recorded in the annals of Plymouth Colony. A Leonard Chester and his wife Mary (family name unknown) do appear in the records of Massachusetts beginning in 1633, the year of Daniel's arrival. Leonard Chester was from Leicestershire, the son of John Chester who married Dorothy Hooker at Birstall do Blaby, Leicestershire, on June 1, 1609. Ruth could not have been a daughter of Leonard and Mary Chester, however, as Leonard was born ca. 1610. He would not have reached the age of consent until 1629, and Ruth was born in 1627 based on the record of her death in 1694 at age of 67.

Could Leonard's parents John and Dorothy have had a daughter Ruth born in England ca. 1627 that traveled to the colonies with her brother and later married Daniel Cole? There is no record of a Ruth in that family. If there had been a daughter named Ruth, we would know it. Dorothy (Hooker) Chester was the sister of the Rev. Thomas Hooker who fled to Holland in 1631 and sailed from there to Massachusetts on the <u>Griffin</u>, July 10, 1633. His family line is very well researched, as his sermons and actions caused him to be recognized as one of the founding fathers of democracy in America (49, pp. 28-31) No Ruth Chester is named.

Based on exhaustive research into all available information, it is reasonable to conclude that Ruth Cole was <u>not</u> a Hopkins. That family has been researched thoroughly and no Ruth of the right age appears. She was <u>not</u> Ruth Collier, as that family is also well researched and William Collier had no daughter by that name. She could have been Ruth Chandler <u>only</u> if family records misidentified the birth order of Edmond's children, an unlikely occurrence. She <u>may</u> have been Ruth Chester as many authors ascribe, but this has yet to be confirmed based on primary evidence.

Tragically, we may never know the lineage of Ruth, the matriarch who was so important to this branch of the Cole family in America. What is known is that she was the faithful wife of Daniel for more than 50 years who nurtured and raised their 11 children under difficult and harsh conditions. Ruth died on December 15, 1694 at age 67, one week before Daniel died at age 80.

**FAMILY LINEAGE –
THE FIRST ELEVEN
GENERATIONS, WITH
HOPKINS FAMILY TIES**

Stephen Hopkins
b. ca, 1582,
d. July1644
(On Mayflower, 1620)

1ˢᵗ wife Mary _____
d. May 1613 in
England.

Nicholas Snow
b Jan. 25, 1599
d. Nov. 15, 1676
(On Ann, 1623)

Constance Hopkins
b. May, 1606,
d. Oct.1677
(On Mayflower, 1620)

Stephen Snow
b. ca. 1636,
d. Dec. 17, 1705

Susanna (Deane)
Rogers
b. ca. 1634,
d. ca.1701

Daniel Cole
b. ca. 1614; d. Dec. 21, 1694
(Arrived from England, 1633)

Ruth (last name unkn.)
b. ca 1627; d. Dec. 15, 1694

William Cole
b. Sept. 15, 1663; d. ca.1737

Hannah **(Hopkins)** Snow
b. Jan. 2 1666; d. June 23, 1737

Elisha Cole
b. Jan. 26, 1688/89; d. ca. 1719

Anne (last name and dates unkn.)

Elisha Cole, Jr.
b. 1719; d. ca. 1801

Hannah Smalley
b. ca. Mar. 1, 1731; d. 1811

Joseph Cole
b. Jan. 11, 1746; d. Feb. 24, 1814

Rebecca Berry
b. Jan. 21, 1752; d. Feb. 15, 1801

Joseph Cole, Jr.
b. Oct. 29, 1775; d. Mar. 9, 1855

Phebe Frost
b. Jan. 28, 1776; d. May 26, 1862

Ira Cole
b. Mar. 15, 1804; d. Mar. 3, 1877

Nancy Bailey
b. Apr. 7, 1807; d. Nov. 16, 1868

Charles Lewis Cole
b. Mar. 21, 1842; d. Feb. 4, 1919

Sarah Almira Woodruff
b. Apr. 22, 1842; d. Jan. 26, 1911

Frank Gerry Cole
b. Nov. 16, 1866; d. Nov. 1, 1939

Rose Belle Kimmich
b. May 17, 1871; d. Feb. 22, 1957

Stuart Gottlieb Cole
b. Nov. 21, 1902; d. Mar. 13, 1987

Doris Mary Lyons
b. Jan. 17, 1905; d. Feb. 4, 1973

David Charles Cole
b. Sept. 22, 1936; d._____

Nancy Carol Murray
b. Nov. 21, 1942; d._____

THE FIRST ELEVEN
GENERATIONS

The following narrative chronology records births, deaths, and marriages in the line of Daniel Cole leading from his son William to the author. Information on many such family events before 1909 were initially collected in Joseph Curtis' book, *Descendants of Elisha Cole*. (19) Curtis' work relied heavily on Frank T. Cole's 1887 research recorded in his book, *Early Genealogy of the Cole Families in America*. (15) Most family details found in the two works appear to have been taken in a fairly scholarly manner from available civil and church records, family Bibles, and interviews with family members. Information drawn from these two works is used here without reference. Insofar as possible, details have been confirmed and numerous errors have been corrected here based on my own research.

Great use has also been made of records collected by the Descendants of Daniel Cole Society, particularly as they relate to the first two generations. Other frequently used sources include the reference collections available at the General Society of Mayflower Descendants; Library of Congress; Daughters of the American Revolution Library in Washington; and the New England Genealogical Society in Boston.

It is important to be faithful to the dates surrounding important family events. This is not an uncomplicated task. The old style Julian calendar was in use at the time of the Plymouth Plantation. The calendar year began on March 25 and ended on March 24 of the succeeding year. March was the first month, December was the tenth, and February was the twelfth. Because some parts of Europe (but not England) had already adopted the Gregorian calendar in use today, the New England colonists began using a two-year dating system between January 1 and March 24 (e.g. January 27, 1699/70) Though this practice adequately defines the year in either dating system, it does not consider the fact that the Julian calendar was 10 days behind the Gregorian calendar until March 1, 1699/1700.

To translate Plymouth Colony dates to the new calendar, it is necessary to add 10 days. For example, the Mayflower Compact was signed on November 11, 1620, which is November 21, 1620, in the new style. (53, pp. 29-30) Elisha Cole Sr. was born January 26, 1688/89, in the old style, but February 5, 1689, in the new. As this paper is drawn from a variety of sources, it is not always possible to know whether a date between January and March 24 in any year before 1700 is in the old or new style. The date recorded here is as found in the most reliable document. Dates do not always agree in various sources, causing the researcher to rely heavily on primary documents when selecting dates that are most reliable or probable.

The spelling of names in public and family records is frequently inconsistent (e.g., Hepziebah, Hepzibah, etc.). That used in the most reliable source is applied. It helps to keep in mind that there were no dictionaries in general use in the 17th Century and no formal rules for spelling. If the spelling allowed the person of the time to understand the intended message or the name, it served its purpose. (53, p. 4)

Commonly used genealogical abbreviations are found in the summaries that follow, but are not applied in narrative text: b. for born; m. for married; d. for died; d.y. for died young; d. unm. for died unmarried; b. for date of birth; ca. for about; s. for son; dau. for daughter; wid. for widow, etc. Two-letter Post Office abbreviations are used for state names in most cases.

An Arabic identification number is given to every generation and bold facing assigned to each child whose history is carried forward. Children are listed in the order of their birth.

The details to follow may be too much for some to grapple with and it would be understandable if they took a speedier course by concentrating solely on those in the direct line, found in boldface. Information on brothers and sisters is included, however, for the benefit those who are more detail oriented and interested in such things as the occurrence of certain given names, and the personal lives and longevity of all closely related family members.

1st Generation

Daniel (b. ca. 1614, d. December 21, 1694) m. ca. 1643 Ruth (_____) (b. ca. 1627, d. December 15, 1694). He represents the first generation in this line of the Cole family in America. Five of their children (John, Israel, Mary, William, and Daniel) married Mayflower descendants, as did many of their children. All in these family lines are eligible for membership in the Society of

Mayflower Descendants and the Jamestowne (sic) Society. Daniel and his wife Ruth had:

John, b. Yarmouth, July 15, 1644; m. at Eastham, December 12, 1666, Ruth Snow, dau. of Nicholas and Constance (Hopkins) Snow, b. Eastham 1644. Subsequent generations are Mayflower descendants. They had two s., John and Joseph, and five dau., Ruth, Hephzebah (Hepzibah), Hannah, Mary and Sarah. John's wife Ruth d. Eastham, January 27, 1716/17 and John d. Eastham, January 6, 1724/25. He held the rank of Lieutenant in the militia and was a man of considerable wealth at the time of his death, leaving lands in Eastham, Harwich, and Truro, plus "meat cattle, horses, kind sheep, and swine and other creatures" to his children. He "saved out" one cow for his former servant Samuel King. (74)

Timothy, b. Eastham (as were all the later children), September 15, 1646. He m. (1) Ruth Smith, likely the mother of his two children, about whom no details have been found. Following her death, he m. (2) widow Martha (Harding) Brown b. 1662, 16 years his junior. No m. dates have been found. He had two s., Timothy and Daniel, likely by his first wife. Timothy, Sr. was one of the East Grantees of Narragansett Township and served in King Philip's War (1675) under Capt. John Gorham of Yarmouth. In 1727, he was awarded 30 acres (Lot 41) in Gorhamtown (now Gorham), ME. He never occupied the land and deeded it to his son Timothy who later sold it to his brother-in-law, Joseph Brown. His s. Daniel m. Sarah Hubbard and d. y., naming his brother Timothy as guardian for two minor children he had by Sarah: Daniel and Elinor. No date is known for the deaths of Timothy, Sr., Jr., or Daniel. (74)

Hepzeibah, b. April 16, 1649; m. (1) May 24, 1677, widower George Crisp He d. July 28, 1682, when their two dau. Mary and Mercy were three and nine months old. She m. (2) widower Daniel Doane, b. Plymouth, ca. 1636, s. of Deacon John and Abigail Doane. He had "at least" 10 children by his first m. and had settled at Eastham by 1645. He was a prominent man, the first physician of Eastham and owner of much land. Hepzeibah and Daniel Doane had one dau., Hepzeibah, b. 1686, at which point he would have been 50 and she 37. Their single child apparently suffered some defect, as his will notes "my daughter Hepzeibah by the Providence of the Allwise God is not endowed with such a competency of understanding as to be capable of supporting and providing for herself". He makes special provisions in his will for her future welfare. He d. December

20, 1712, in his 76th year. No date has been found for the death of his wife, but she must have outlived him as she is named in his will, the wording of which provides insight into the position women held in society at the time. Even possessions shared in marriage were not their own: "I give my Loving Wife Hepsibah the bed whereon we commonly Lye with the Bedstead and furniture thereunto belonging. the Curtains, Bedcord, a pair of sheets, a Coverlid, and blanket bolster and pillows, also all her wearing apparell to be enjoyed to herself". He also left her half of the land on which the home stood and the dwelling's "eastern end from the foundation to the roof". The other half he willed to a son from the first marriage that was also living there at the time. (74)

Ruth, b. April 15, 1651; m. (1) John, b. Plymouth, November 16, 1649, s. of John and Abigail (Howland) Young. It is believed their dau. Mercy and a s. Benjamin m. children of Stephen Snow and Joseph Snow, the issue of both marriages therefore being descendants of Mayflower passenger Stephen Hopkins. John d. 1718 and Ruth m. (2) in 1720, Capt. Jonathan Bangs b. February 25, 1669/70, s. of Edward and Rebecca Bangs. Ruth was his third wife. There is no record of issue from this m. He d. at Brewster, Cape Cod, November 9, 1728. No record of her death has been found.

Israel, b. January 8 or June 8, 1653; m. April 24, 1679, Mary (Paine) Rogers, widow of James Rogers (s. of Joseph Rogers of the Mayflower). Mary was the dau. of Thomas and Mary (Snow) Paine, Jr. Mary Snow was the granddau. of Nicholas and Constance (Hopkins) Snow, a Mayflower passenger. Mary had three children by James Rogers before his death, April 13, 1678: Samuel (later called James), Mary, and Abigail. Their dau. Mary m. John Cole, Jr., s. of Daniel and Ruth's s. John and subsequent generations are Mayflower descendants. Israel Cole and the widow Rogers had three children: Hannah, Israel, and Isaac. All subsequent generations are Mayflower descendants. Israel was an Eastham representative to the General Court of Massachusetts at Boston in 1698. He d. January 21, 1723/4, the wealthiest man in the county at the time. No record of Mary's death has been found.

James, b. November 30, 1655; m. January 10, 1683/4, Hannah Childs, whose parents are unkn. James and Hannah had: Mary, b. September 14, 1684; Ruth, b. November 13, 1686 (d. at birth); James, b. November 25, 1693; Samuel, b. December 22, 1695; Ruth, b. November 16, 1698 (their second child by that name as the Ruth, b. 1686, was deceased); and Martha, b. July 1, 1700. He was a fisherman and d.

sometime before February 4, 1717/18, at which point his property was distributed through a letter of administration. He may have d. unexpectedly at sea, which could explain the lack of a will. Whaling and fishing were major industries in the area. (74)

Mary, b. March 10, 1658; m. May 26, 1681, Joshua Hopkins, b. June 1657, the seventh child of Giles and Catherine (Wheldon) Hopkins. Subsequent generations are Mayflower descendants. They had eight children: John, Abigael, Elisha, Liddiah, Mary, Joshua, Hannah, and Phebe. He and Mary settled on the east side of Town Cove near his father's house. Joshua was a farmer, having inherited a large estate from his father, and was "the most opulent man of the time." She d. March 1, 1733/34, and is buried in the Orleans churchyard. He d. August 1738.

Hester (Esther), b. ca. 1661; m. ca. 1684, Medad Atwood, b. January 16, 1658/59, s. of Stephen and Abigail (Dunham) Atwood. They had seven children: Mercy, Abigail, David, Samuel, Esther, Phebe, and Nathan (or Nathaniel). No date of her death has been found, but it is known to be after 1735, as she is named in the will of her brother Daniel signed that year.

William, b. September 15, 1663.

Daniel, b. September 1666; m. before October 1, 1695, to Mercy Fuller, the dau. of the Rev. Samuel and Elizabeth (Bowen) Fuller of Middleboro. Mercy was a granddau. of Samuel Fuller Sr., who accompanied his father Edward on the Mayflower. They had no children. She d. September 25, 1735, in her 63rd year. He d. Eastham, June 15, 1736, in his 69th year. His will left his goods to his living brother William and sister Hester, as well as the heirs of his deceased brothers and sisters. Only his sister Ruth is unnamed, indicating she had likely died. There is no indication why Daniel did not leave something to Ruth's heirs. The introduction to his will is common of the times and confirms the religious nature of the Cole family: *In the Name of God, Amen, being weak and very Infirmed in Body but of perfect mind and memory thanks be given to God, therefore calling to mind the mortality of my Body and knowing that it is appointed for all men once to dye do make and ordain this, my last will and testament, that is to say principally the first of all I give and Recommend my Soul unto the hands of God that gave it and my body I recommend to the earth to be buried in Decent Christian Burial at the Discission of my Executor nothing doubting but at the General Resurrection I shall receive the same again by the mighty power of God and as touching such worldly estate as herewith it hath pleased God to bless me in this life . . .* (74)

Thomas, b. ca. 1669; m. date unkn. Lydia Remick, b. February 8, 1676, dau. of Christian and Hannah (Thompson?) Remick of Kittery, ME. Christian came from England or Holland and was a "planter, surveyor, selectman, and treasurer of the town at Eliot Neck." Thomas and Lydia had at least four s. and three dau. between 1680 and 1717: Remick, Robert, Abner, Hazael (Asahael), Jerusha, Ariel, and Charity. They may also have had a s. Daniel, b. ca. 1696, and a dau. Hannah, b. ca. 1698. Thomas was a Freeman at Eastham. In 1717 he removed to Portsmouth, NH, and is later shown as a storekeeper and mariner in Kittery, ME. He d. September/October 1725. He was survived by his wife, Lydia, whose date of death is unknown. (74)

2nd Generation

William *(Daniel^1)* married at Eastham, December 2, 1686, Hannah Snow, born there January 2, 1666, dau. of Stephen and Susanna (Deane-Rogers) Snow. Stephen Snow of Eastham was the son of Nicholas and Constance (Hopkins) Snow, and grandson of Stephen Hopkins of the <u>Mayflower</u>. Subsequent members of the Cole family in this hereditary line are <u>Mayflower</u> descendants. Susanna was the daughter of Stephen and Elizabeth (Ring) Deane and widow of Joseph Rogers. Stephen Deane arrived on the <u>Fortune</u> in 1621.

William and Hannah lived at Eastham where she d. June 23, 1737. No record has been found of William's death, probably at Eastham, known to be after November 20, 1735 (ca. 1737).
William and Hannah had:

Elisha, b. January 26, 1688/89.
David, b. October 4, 1691; m. at Eastham, October 7, 1725, Jerusha Doane, b. at Eastham January 23, 1704/05, dau. of Isaac and Margaret (Atwood) Doane. They had daus. Vashty, Jerusha, and Hannah; and s. William and David. He d. at Eastham before January 21, 1735, when his estate was administered. His widow Jerusha m. (2) at Eastham, June 13, 1740, John Young, a descendent of Stephen Hopkins. There is no record of issue. She d. at Wellfleet, February 25, 1792, and is buried in Duck Creek Cemetery there.
Hannah, b. at Eastham, December 15, 1693; m. at Truro, February 26, 1718/19, Elisha Doane, b. Provincetown, ca. 1699, s. of Hezekiah and Hannah (Snow) Doane. He was a prominent businessman, owning several whaling ships.
    Their children were Joseph, Elisha, Hannah, and Rachel who m. (1) John Wormley and (2) the Hon. Edward Bacon. Elisha Doane

d. at Wellfleet December 7, 1759, at age 60. As an interesting glimpse into family relationships, Elisha was apparently displeased with Rachel's first husband, as his will reads in part: *To my daughter Rachel and her heirs and assigns forever, one fifth part of my estate . . . discharged so that no part of the estate either real or personal herein given to my daughter Rachel may or shall be in any sort liable or subject to the control, intermedling, debts, forfeiture or engagement of John Wormley.* (74) Hannah d. at Wellfleet February 25, 1786 in her 95th year.

Jane, b. January 4, 1695/96; m. (1) Thomas Gross at Eastham December 7, 1721, s. of Simon and Mary (Bond) Gross. He d. between November 8, 1725, and March 14, 1727/28. Jane m. (2) at Eastham May 16, 1734, Joseph Smalley b. ca. 1696, twice a widower. Her children were Hannah (Gross), b. November 8, 1725, who m. Samuel Smalley; and Jane (Smalley), b. ca. April 19, 1735.

3rd Generation

Elisha *(William^2, Daniel^1)* married Anne, otherwise unidentified. Information on both Anne and Elisha is incomplete. There is no record of their marriage, but it is believed to have been before the winter of 1714 based on the birth dates of their children recorded in Eastham as being "of Elisha and Anne Cole." Her family name and the year of her death are unknown. The Daniel Cole Society lists Elisha's year of death as 1719, only a few years after their marriage and in the birth year of their last child. The early death of Elisha, Sr. at age 30, in a family where the male progenitors lived an average of 72 years, hints that an accident or sudden illness of some kind claimed his life. Elisha and Anne had:

Joshua, "the s. of Elisha and Anne Cole, was b. at Eastham October 9, 1715". He m. Hannah Cole, a cousin, dau. of his uncle David and Jerusha (Doane) Cole.

Eunice, b. November 24, 1717; m. Silas Pierce. No record of issue.

Mary, b. ca. 1718.

Elisha, Jr., b. January 26, 1719.

4th Generation

Elisha, Jr., *(Elisha^3, William^2, Daniel^1)* m. (1) Priscilla Smalley (Smale, Smally, Smallee) at Eastham, December 13, 1739. Eastham records dated September 4, 1739, state:

"Then entered the intention of Elisha Cole Jr. and Priscilla Smalee, both of Eastham, to proceed in marriage." Under date December 13, 1739: *"Then Elisha Cole Jr. and Priscilla Smally, both of Eastham, were married in Eastham by me, Isaiah Lewes, Minister."*

Priscilla was the daughter of Joseph Smalley and his second wife Mercy. Joseph Smalley married (1) Priscilla Young of Eastham, April 24, 1718. She died April 1, 1719, perhaps giving birth to a child. Three months later Joseph Smalley married (2) Mercy Young of Eastham (not sister to Priscilla Young) on July 9, 1719. She died August 2, 1733, and he married (3) Jane Cole, also of Eastham, May 16, 1734. Jane was the daughter of William and Hannah (Snow) Cole and aunt to Elisha, Jr. (5, p. 246)

Priscilla (Smalley) Cole was born April 8, 1720, the first child from the union of Joseph and Mercy (Young) Smalley. Priscilla d. in 1740 at age 19, likely at childbirth shortly after she married Elisha, Jr. The following year Elisha, Jr., married (2) Hannah Smalley, thought to be a cousin of Priscilla.

In the autumn of 1746 Elisha, Jr., and Hannah moved from Cape Cod's south shore to Dutchess County, New York. Hannah's father and his family moved to this area a year or two earlier and apparently passed word back that the land was suitable for farming.

We do not know the route the young family took. The journey likely started over water from Harwich on Cape Cod to the Connecticut or Housatonic River where they moved up river, and then overland across the rolling hills of western Connecticut and the Tacontic Mountains into New York. The site they chose to build a log house was by a stream that is today the outlet of Barrrett's Pond near the present town of Kent. Elisha's aunt Mary, the unmarried sister of Elisha, Sr., relocated with the family.

Elisha, Jr., and Hannah had three sons at the time of their arrival in Dutchess County: Elisha, Nathan, and Joseph. Five daughters and three more sons were born in the years after they settled. Hannah was therefore the mother of all Elisha's children, except perhaps his first-born Joshua, who did not move to New York with the family. Joshua is assumed to have been Elisha, Jr's. only child by his first wife Priscilla who died from complications at childbirth, causing the child Joshua to remain behind with her relatives.

The area they chose was in the heights east of the Hudson River. It was owned by Adolphe Philipse who had purchased it from Dutch speculators at the end of the 17th Century. Settlers soon flowed to the area from New England, Long Island, and northern Westchester and became tenants on the land. The tenants gained ownership after the Revolution when the Philipse family, who were Tories, was forced to forfeit its possessions and holdings.

Elisha, Jr., was a tenant farmer working land on the slopes of the Tacontic Mountains. It was not flat or fertile as had been the case on Cape Cod, but undulating, peppered with rock outcroppings, and covered by forest. It was rugged, inhospitable terrain. Elisha cleared land for subsistence crops and built a log house for his family near the stream at the outlet of Barrett's Pond in the present town of Kent. In 1748 he built a carding mill and a gristmill there, and it came to be known as Cole's Mill. He also established a sawmill on the East Branch of the Croton River.

The land had belonged to Roger Morris, son-in-law of Frederick Philipse. It was confiscated by the State of New York and sold to Elisha by the Commissioners of Forfeiture on June 11, 1782. "The parcel containing 396 acres, more or less, sold in consideration of £234 9-1." (19, p. 26). Records of the Descendants of Daniel Cole Society note he purchased another 513 acres in 1788, further dividing and adding land for his sons to farm as they married and established families. (74)

A mill was in operation on or near the site of the first mill and owned by members of the Cole family until 1888, when New York City purchased it for reservoir purposes. The reservoir was started August 27, 1890, and completed in 1896. Water soon covered the mill area, but substantial farmland was preserved for use by the family. The following description of the Cole's Mill property is found in the 1888 condemnation proceedings: House, one story and attic; barn, 21'x 32'; carding mill (for combing wool) 36'x 20'; saw mill, 13'x 46'; gristmill, 21'x 22'.

There is hardly an old family in Putnam County that has not intermarried with the Coles. The marriage of first and second cousins was frequent, and in one instance a Cole became, by marriage, the aunt to her own cousins.

Elisha, Jr., and his family contributed to the early progress of the communities in which they lived by participating in local government, the Baptist church, and devotion to their families and farms. Elisha was a Baptist preacher. He was one of the original nine members of the first Baptist church founded there November 16, 1751, and its first leader. (40, p. 317) His son Nathan was an Elder in the church in Carmel, preaching in the open air in the summer and in homes during the winter. The society had no building of its own until ca. 1780. Elisha's son Daniel was later a Deacon of the church and his son Ebenezer both a Deacon and the Pastor.

Mt. Carmel Baptist was the first church in Carmel. The 1780 church had nothing but benches, not even a pulpit. It served the greater areas of Kent, Putnam Valley, Southeast, and Patterson as the sole Baptist church in the community. This building also functioned as the local meetinghouse until a new building was erected in 1806. When Putnam County split from Dutchess County in 1812, included in the Act of the State Legislature was a notation that the Mt. Carmel Church building was to be used as a Courthouse until one was erected in 1814. In 1836, a new church building was erected and it served until 1870 when the present building was completed.

Elisha was a Captain in the 7th Regt. of the Dutchess County Militia under the command of Col. Henry Ludington during the American Revolution. His commission in the rank of Captain confirms he was a man of stature and means.

Elisha was partly paralyzed and "somewhat demented" before his death ca. 1801 at age 82. Hannah's mental powers "gave way" also, while physically she was very strong. She d. in 1811 at age 80. Elisha and Hannah had:

Joshua, b. ca. 1740; d. February 3, 1826. (Likely the s. of Elisha's first wife, Priscilla).

Elisha, b. January 26, 1743 (also appears as September 3, 1742); m. 1763, Charity, b. 1744, dau. of Caleb and Sarah (Hamblin) Hazen. The Hazen family moved to the area from Norwich ca. 1740. Elisha bought a farm of 513 acres from the Committee of Forfeiture, August 30, 1788. This land is near Long Pond in the present town of Carmel, Putnam County, NY. She d. 1811. He d. February 3, 1826, at age 83. Elisha and Charity are buried in the family plot on what was their farm. Elisha was a Private in the 7th Regt., Dutchess County Militia under Col. Henry Ludington, as were his father Elisha and three brothers, including Joseph. (81, p. 150.) Charity's line can be traced back 18 generations to Henry II, King of England (1154-1189). Those who follow in the line of Elisha are eligible for membership in the Illegitimate Sons and Daughters of the Kings of Britain (the Royal Bastards).

Nathan, b. 1744. He was licensed to preach by the Baptist church in Carmel on May 2, 1772. On removal of the church in May 1773 to North East Town, members not moving organized into a church by themselves with Nathan Cole as their pastor. Among those remaining was his father Elisha Sr.. On December 12, 1791, the church agreed to pay to Elder Nathan C. Cole £12 for the following year. He preached for 30 years and was 59 when he d. February 6, 1803, after only one day of sickness.

Joseph, b. January 11, 1746.

Eunice, b. January 1748; m. (1) Hackaliah, s. of Joseph Merritt. He d. and she m. (2) Nathan Crosby. He was a Private, 3rd Regt., Dutchess County Militia in the Revolution. He d. October 27, 1805, at age 72. She d. January 17, 1821, age 73.

Daniel, b. November 26, 1749. He was an ordained Deacon in the Baptist church in Carmel. He d. December 10, 1834, at age 85

Hannah, b. 1751; m. Freeman, b. 1754, s. of Jonathan and Rebecca (Freeman) Hopkins. She d. March 31, 1802 at age 51. He d. March 31, 1830 at age 76. He was a member of the 7th Regt., Dutchess County Militia and later a Baptist preacher.

Naomi, b. 1753; m. Jesse Smith. His parents and dob. unkn. She d. 1794. He d. 1825. He was b. Putnam County, was a member of the 7th Regt., Dutchess County Militia, and was present at the capture of Stony Point by Anthony Wayne. Their s., Charles G. Smith, m. Margaret, a dau. of his uncle Ebenezer Cole and wife Mary.

Ebenezer, b. 1754: m. Mary Ogden. He served in the Revolution in Col. Ludington's Regiment, was a deacon and later a pastor in the Baptist church, and performed the marriage ceremony for each of his 12 children. He d. August 18, 1815.

Priscilla Ann, b. 1756; m. Gen. James Townsend, b. 1756, s. of Charles Townsend. He d. Carmel, March 13, 1832, in his 76th year. She d. there June 11, 1839, in her 83rd year. He was a grandson of Elisha Townsend who was b. at Oyster Bay, August 1704, and d. North Salem, July 1805. James was a prominent man and a member of the 7th Regt., Dutchess County Militia. He was a Lieutenant Colonel in the 6th Regt. Dutchess County Militia in the War of 1812 and, by November 9, 1812, a Brigadier General in the 30th Infantry Brigade in Dutchess County. He remained such until February 3, 1817, when he resigned his command.

Mercy, b. 1757; m. Tracy, b. September 8, 1756, s. of Mary (Tracy) Ballard. Mercy d. February 8, 1826 at age 69. He was a Private, 7th Regt., Dutchess County Militia and d. in Carmel January 4, 1829, at age 72.

John, b. October 6, 1761; m. _____ Ogden. He was one of three sons of Elisha, Jr., Cole who m. Ogden sisters. He d. September 24, 1850.

5th Generation

Joseph (Elisha, Jr.,[4] Elisha[3], William[2], Daniel[1]) was born January 11, 1746, at Cole's Mills, in the town of Kent. He married on date unknown but before April 1769 (1) Rebecca, born January 21, 1752, daughter of Jabez Berry. She could have been no more than 17 years of age at the time of the marriage and was the mother of his 12 children. She died February 15, 1801, at age 49 and is buried in the Cole farm cemetery near Long Pond. He married on date unknown (2) Susan (Berry) Chase, born March 15, 1744, widow of Obediah Chase who died July 4, 1799. She was probably an older sister of Joseph's first wife. They had no issue. Each had 11 children at the time of this marriage, meaning one of Joseph and Rebecca's children had already died.

Joseph Cole was a member of the 7th Regt. in the Dutchess County Militia. Joseph's father Elisha, Jr., and brothers Daniel, Elisha, and Ebenezer also joined in the Revolution, a struggle that lasted from 1775 to 1783. Even Joseph's young nephew, Reuben, was involved before the conflict ended. (19) They were all Privates assigned to the 7th Regiment (Infantry). The Commander was Col. Henry Ludington (also spelled Ludenton and Ludinton by Curtis, and both Ludinton and Ludington in Joseph's pay records).

There were seven regiments of militia in Dutchess County. One regiment, the "Associated Exempts", was composed of men between 50 and 60 years of age who were to be called out only "in time of invasion". The 7th Regiment was composed principally of residents of what are now the towns of Kent and Carmel.

The militia was called out when wanted and kept as long as needed, and the soldiers were then sent home. Sometimes a regiment or part of a regiment would be called out half a dozen times during a year, for a week or so at a time. In New York the militiamen were involved in many hotly contested fights. Members of the Cole family probably performed splendidly when called upon, but there is no detailed record of their service.

The Colonel commanding a militia regiment was responsible for seeing that each member presented himself when "warned" and was equipped with a blanket, flintlock rifle or musket, powder horn, and a flint, and often a tomahawk. A Private received monthly one pound of sugar, two ounces of tea, some tobacco and $6.66 in pay. However, the nation was young and poor so final pay for their effort was not received until well after the end of the conflict. On April 27, 1784, the Legislature passed an act for such payments and the State Treasurer was required to issue certificates of indebtedness bearing 5 percent interest to persons to whom payment was due, or their legal representatives. Such certificates could be used in payment of taxes, purchase of forfeited estates, etc.

Joseph returned to his family after the war, worked his land, raised livestock, and remained active in the Baptist church until he died on February 24, 1814, at age 68. He is buried in the Cole cemetery next to his first wife Rebecca who died February 15, 1801, at age 49. His second wife Susan died in 1836 at age 92. Joseph and Rebecca had:

Berry, b. February 24, 1769; d. May 29, 1835.
William, b. 1771; d. unm. and likely at a young age.

Susannah, b. September 23, 1773; m. Henry, b. Reading, CT, December 12, 1769, s. of Josiah and Elizabeth (Bouton) Nichols. They lived in Kent, Dutchess County, NY. He d. February 10, 1849 at age 79. She d. October 2, 1856 at age 83. Josiah Nichols was a cavalry officer in the Revolution.

Anna, b. 1775; m. Charles Green.

Joseph, b. October 29, 1775.

Samuel, b. December 24, 1777; moved from Carmel to western New York in 1835, and later to Livingston County, MI, as one of the first settlers of that region; d. March 26, 1851.

Nathan, b. August 17, 1780; d. February 10, 1877. He was a farmer and Deacon of the Baptist church. He resettled from Kent to Covert, NY, near Cayuga Lake.

Ruth, b. January 19, 1783; m. September 12, 1801, Alvin, b. Kent, October 4, 1778, s. of Obediah and Susan (Berry) Chase. She d. April 17, 1832, in her 49th year and he m. (2) September 16, 1832, Martha Elizabeth, b. Kent, 1789, dau. of David and Clara Northrup (Kelley) Dingee. He d. February 26, 1853, in Pawling, NY. She d. October 23, 1857, in Fishkill, NY.

Asahel, b. May 31, 1786; d. October 23, 1875.

Cynthia, b. September 4, 1788; m. December 6, 1809, Enos, b. March 1, 1789, s. of Jeremiah and Thankful (Stone) Hopkins. He d. March 23, 1859, at age 70. She d. April 1, 1864 at age 75.

Levi Hall, b. July 1, 1791; m. December 3, 1814, by Elder Ebenezer Cole to Hannah, b. January 16, 1798, dau. of Daniel and Susan (Ogden) Cole. She was his cousin. In his early married life he lived on what was called Cole's Street, the highway leading from Cole's Mill to Mahopac. He later purchased a farm in the southwest part of town of Carmel on which he lived until his death. For many years he was a Deacon of the Baptist church at Red Mills. He was reportedly a good neighbor, a respected citizen, and a zealous Christian. He d. October 17, 1860, at age 69. She d. December 16, 1876, at age 78.

Ramah, b. February 27, 1795; m. (1) Esther Mills, (2) Cynthia Martin and (3) Lucy Winans. Ramah settled at Ovid, NY. He moved from there about 1824 to the east half of section 24 in Troy, Oakland Co., Michigan. He afterward moved to Shiawassee Co. His wife Esther d. at Troy in 1826. During the winter of 1825-26, he taught in a log schoolhouse. The benches in the schoolhouse were made from basswood logs split through the center, flat side up, and raised from the floor by legs inserted in the under side with no cushions and no backs. The school was warmed by wood in a Dutch fireplace where half a dozen boys and girls would be standing in turn trying to warm themselves. Later he kept a hotel and helped many new settlers with gratuitous meals and lodging. He d. near Byron, Michigan, May 31, 1865, at age 70.

6th Generation

Joseph, Jr. (*Joseph^5, Elisha, Jr.,^{4}, Elisha^3, William^2, Daniel^1*) married in Carmel, February 2, 1797, Phebe, b. January 28, 1776, daughter of David and Sarah (Hyatt) Frost. The ceremony was conducted in the Frost home with Joseph's brother Nathan officiating. He was 21 and she 20 at the time of their marriage.

Joseph Cole, Jr., served in the War of 1812. Congress declared war on June 18, 1812. The British succeeded in taking Washington, but were defeated on New York's Lake Champlain in September 1814, and stopped at Fort McHenry in Baltimore harbor during the same month. The Treaty of Ghent officially ended the war on December 24, 1814. Unaware of the signing, Andrew Jackson decisively defeated British forces at New Orleans on January 8, 1815.

War muster and company payroll records show Joseph Cole, Jr., was a Corporal and Fifer in an Infantry Company of the 1st Regiment, New York Detached Militia, from August 18 to December 3, 1814. His term of service for that period would have been three months and 16 days at $10 per month, for a total of $35.32. Details of his service have not been uncovered, except that he was assigned to Harlem Heights, NY. Records showing his application for bounty land under the Act of September 28, 1850, indicate he had only one month of service, from August 18 to September 20, 1814, and was discharged at "Brooklin". This was enough to earn a bounty for 40 acres, which he received. He apparently never took up the land and probably sold his right to it before his death.

Just as his grandfather Elisha, Jr., had moved west from Cape Cod to Dutchess County in search of good farmland and opportunity, Joseph relocated his family westward to central New York State. He settled in the village of Beaver Dams, Town of Dix, in the present Schuyler County ca. 1833, at which time he would have been 57. Joseph and Phebe's sons Charles and Ira preceded them to Beaver Dams in 1830. No record has been found to confirm he owned his own farm, and Joseph and Phebe may have moved into one of the log homes built by their sons Ira and Charles. They no doubt joined their sons and daughters-in-law in working the land as a family enterprise, and contributed to the building of Ira's new and much larger home.

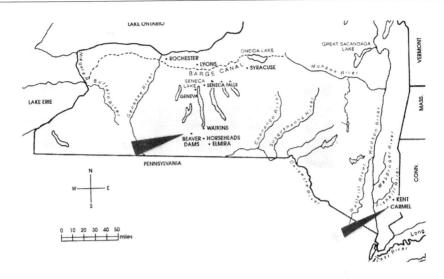

Cole Family Relocation within New York State, 1830

Beaver Dams was so named because there were two beaver dams on Post Creek at the north end of the village site. First called Beaver Dams in 1843, it was formerly the village of West Catlin in the Town of Dix.

Joseph was among the earliest settlers in the area. He was chosen Moderator of the First Universalist Society of Dix organized on February 26, 1848. There were 22 constituent members, and an edifice was erected in 1853 for $1,500. Membership reached 60, but the congregation found itself without a minister for a period of 10 years. The society eventually disbanded and vanished from the village history by 1880.

Joseph Cole, Jr., died in Beaver Dams on March 9, 1855 at age 79. His wife Phebe appeared before a justice of the peace on May 15 of that year stating that the original bounty of "forty acres" Joseph had been awarded for his service in the Revolutionary had "since been legally disposed of and cannot now be returned". She applied for additional bounty land to which she believed she was entitled as his widow under the Act of March 8, 1855. She signed the application with an X. The issue was still unresolved in 1857 when she declared that she had not yet received a warrant for land. It is believed the funds available for land grants were expended before her application was approved, and her petition was never honored. (67)

According to the Chemung County census of 1860 she was still living with her son Ira, his wife Nancy, and their two sons on the family farm. Phebe died there May 26, 1862, at age 86. Both she and Joseph Cole, Jr., are buried in the Beaver Dams cemetery. Joseph, Jr., and Phebe had:

George Frost, b. December 23, 1797; m. May 5, 1822, Elizabeth Merrick. Tragedy befell them. He d. after only four years of marriage on December 4, 1826 at age 28, and was buried on Cole's farm near Long Pond in the town of Carmel. They had two children, both of whom d. young: an infant dau. "buried October. 5, 1822," five months after they were married and Harry, b. 1824, who started to visit his grand-mother Phebe after she moved to Beaver Dams, was taken sick, returned home, and died.

Charles Green, b. August 14, 1800; m. (1) January 14, 1824, Susan Wood. She d. February 9, 1827, at age 21. They apparently had no issue. He m. (2) February 6, 1830, Mary, b. December 12, 1808, in Brewster, NY, dau. of Samuel and Hannah (Wright) Bailey. Charles and his brother Ira relocated west and farmed 65 1/2 acres near the village of Beaver Dams beginning in 1830. The two brothers worked the land together and lived in a log house with their families for three years. Then Charles built a second log house in the same yard and his family lived there until his death. Charles and Mary had three s. and four dau., all b. in Beaver Dams. He d. at Beaver Dams April 7, 1846, at age 45 when the children ranged in age from less than one year to 12. Mary continued to live in the cabin on a family farm adjacent to her bother-in-law Ira's farm. Mary d. June 17, 1897, at age 88.

Ira, b. March 15, 1804.

Harlem, b. February 4, 1810; d. unm. October 20, 1838.

Asahel, b. June 5, 1814; m. June 23, 1835, Mary Ann, b. Marcellus, NY, June 3, 1817, dau. of Ira and Lavina (Richardson) Savory. He was a farmer. The Savorys came to Beaver Dams from Hartford, CT. Asahel d. Havana, NY, September 25, 1884. Mary d. Moreland, NY, March 21, 1889.

Minerva Ruth, b. August 30, 1817; m. Beaver Dams, October 17, 1843, Uriah, b. Hornby, NY, 1825, s. of George and Phebe (Rockwell) Patchen. He d. 1894. She d. New York City, March 21, 1904.

7th Generation

Ira *(Joseph, Jr.,[6] Joseph[5], Elisha, Jr.,[4] Elisha[3], William[2], Daniel[1])* m. Brewster, NY, March 10-18, 1826, Nancy, b. there April 7, 1807, dau. of Samuel and Hannah (Wright) Bailey. She was the sister of Mary Bailey, wife of Ira's brother Charles Green Cole. The sisters and their husbands cleared and developed the land together.

A barge canal opened on October 26, 1825, linking the Hudson River with Lake Erie. It eased migration to the western parts of New York. It was the route Ira and Charles used as they moved to settle near Beaver Dams in 1830. Their mother Phebe's brother, Underhill Frost, had settled in Beaver Dams earlier, which may account for their decision to relocate there. As noted, their father Joseph Jr., mother Phebe, and brother Asahel followed a few years later.

Ira and Charles traveled via Packet boat from Beacon, NY, where the Fishkill River joins the Hudson River, north and west along the Hudson and Mohawk Rivers to Oneida Lake, then west on the newly-opened barge canal and adjoining canal arteries to Geneva, down Seneca Lake to Watkins, and from there overland to Beaver Dams. The journey took one week.

The 65 1/2 acre Cole farm, purchased from Charles Corroll of Corrollton (ca. 1830), was located in the Town of Catlin south of Beaver Dams in the eastern part of Lot #39, southwest section to Township No. 2. (77) The area where they chose to settle consists of long deep lakes, rolling green hills, and rich soil.

Ira, Charles, and their families farmed and lived together in one log home on the land for three years until Charles completed a separate home for his family to the south on the same parcel. Mary and their seven children continued to live there after Charles d. April 7, 1846. The two log homes no longer exist. The fine home Ira built for his family and parents still rests on the land.

The Town of Catlin is in Chemung County and was formed when the Town of Catherine to the east was divided on April 16, 1823. Catlin itself was divided in 1835, the northern part becoming the Town of Dix, in Schuyler County. The village of Beaver Dams was in the southwest corner of the new township, which also contained the villages of Townsend, Havana (today Montour Falls), Moreland, and Watkins (today Watkins Glen) in the extreme northeast of the township on the southern end of Seneca Lake.

Oral histories suggest a family connection between Ira's wife Nancy (Bailey) Cole and James A. Bailey of Ringling Bros., Barnum & Bailey Circus fame. None is possible, as James was not really a Bailey, but was born James McGinness in 1847 near Pontiac, Michigan. He lost his parents by age seven and was adopted in 1859 by Fred H. Bailey, a circus promoter, taking the Bailey family name then. James m., but died in 1906 without issue. (37, p. 239)

Nancy might have had circus people in her family, however, as Putnam County was the "cradle of the American circus" from the early 19th Century through the 1920s. We find the name Hachaliah Bailey as one prominent in the circus business in Somers, NY, near Brewster where Nancy m. Ira in 1826. (37, p. 126, 239) Hachaliah may have been her uncle, but confirmation of this or any other tie between Nancy and members of the Bailey family involved in circus work is left to a future researcher.

Another possible connection exists. Nancy's mother-in-law, Phebe Frost, was a Hyatt on her mother's side. Hyatt Frost (Nancy's cousin?) was b. 1827 in Putnam County. He went on to manage and later own the Van Amburgh

Circus that traveled extensively in England and the United States. (37, p. 136, 162) Hyatt joined with P.T. Barnum on several business ventures. Interesting as it is to speculate, there is no evidence to date connecting Nancy to Hyatt Frost's circus adventures.

The Cole name was prominent in the circus profession during the period and the Cole Bros. Circus is active today. The most famous Cole in the profession was William Washington Cole, b. 1847, descendant of an English circus family and son of William H. Cole, a renowned contortionist in his day. William was "worth millions" at the time of his death in 1915. (37, p. 289) Alas, he was not part of the line of Coles descending from Daniel.

Map of Schuyler County, New York, 1860

As noted, Ira relocated to Beaver Dams area with his brother Charles in 1830. (73) It is unclear if Nancy and their two children ages two and three traveled with them or joined very soon after. Oral history indicates the wives and children followed once the land had been partially cleared and the first crops were in. This may account for the fact Ira and Charles lived together in a log cabin initially, suitable accommodations for men without their families. Nancy must have joined him by early 1832. She conceived twin daughters in the spring and they were born in Beaver Dams on December 9, 1832. They represent the only occurrence of twins in this line of the Cole family.

Life was not easy for Ira and Nancy as they set about farming and raising a family in their new surroundings. The land had to be cleared before subsistence crops could be planted and initially they had only hand tools to aid in the work. Days were filled with hard physical labor.

Farm Home Built by Ira Cole and Family, 1832/33
(Photographed 2002)

The five-room, two-story home that Ira soon built their remains today at 61 Beaver Dams Road (County Road 19), an extension of Main Street, approximately 3/10 of a mile south of the Schuyler/Chemung County line. Subsequent owners lovingly restored it in the 1990s. (70) The original pine board floors, plaster walls, door hardware, decorative window moldings, kitchen wainscoting and two handmade wooden fireplace hearths are extant. The shale foundation laid and walls raised by the Cole family ca. 1832/33 are intact. Beams and studs cut from trees cleared from the land are partly exposed with ax and saw marks clearly visible, along with the wooden pegs hammered in place to anchor the studs to ceiling joists.

There was a large fireplace for heating and cooking in the kitchen area when the house was built, but the original does not exist today. It appears to have been the only fireplace in the home. Wood-burning potbelly or "Franklin" stoves were likely used to provide heat in the parlor and elsewhere in the living quarters. This explains the existence today of two wooden mantels, without hearths and chimneys, cut and hand-planed by members of the family. The intricately cut molding around the parlor windows speaks to the elegance of the original home.

It is a sizeable house, modified over the years to meet the needs of successive families. An electric pump under the kitchen area still draws water from the 16-foot well dug by members of the Cole family. Modern kitchen appliances, indoor bathrooms, and central heating have been added, but the character of the more than 175-year old home remains. The entryway with its handcrafted door molding, the parlor where the Cole family gathered to entertain and celebrate family events, the steep narrow stairway leading to the second floor, and an expansive upstairs bedroom remain very much as they must have been in the mid-19th Century. Wear marks on the pine floors and doorsills stand as evidence of the daily activity of the two generations of Coles that made the house their home.

He, his wife Nancy, their three sons and three daughters, Ira's mother Phebe, and perhaps his father Joseph Cole, Jr., all lived on the Cole farm and shared the dwelling. Ira and Nancy's son Charles Lewis Cole was born in one of the bedrooms in the spring of 1842. He grew up there, played in the yard, farmed the land with his father, went off to war, and returned to its warmth before marrying Sarah Almira Woodruff.

The clothes they wore were mostly homespun from flax. Meats caught and eaten included deer, bear, raccoon, grouse, pigeon, and rabbit. Homemade tallow candles were used for lighting. When a new school, church or log house was to be built, neighbors from many miles around were invited to attend the "raising". With neighborly help a building was near completion in a single day, after which the housewives served a bountiful supper, generally an ox barbecue with homemade "dainties" prepared by the ladies. After the meal, a dance was held on a large platform erected for the occasion. (25)

Records do not list any contact with the Seneca Indians living in Beaver Dams area, although many returned to the Finger Lakes region after Sullivan's march to open the area to white settlers in 1779. They largely worked as laborers.

By 1879 the hamlet had one general and two grocery stores, one blacksmith, and one wagon shop, a tannery, a copper shop, a shoe shop, one tailor, and two millinery establishments, two churches (one Methodist Episcopal and one Universalist), and a public school. A depot on the Elmira-Jefferson-Canandaigua Rail Road line (later the New York Central) in the southwest corner of town contained an express and telephone office. There was one resident "minister of the Gospel" and one justice of the peace. The population reached nearly 250 in 1880. (25, p. 608)

It is interesting to speculate when and why the Coles in the line, so firmly involved in the Baptist church in Putnam County before relocating west, became Episcopalians. The transition likely occurred in the latter half of the 19th Century when Ira and his family were living in Beaver Dams. There was a Methodist Episcopal Church there, established in 1833, which by 1861 had a structure capable of holding 450 worshipers, seating about 100. (25, p. 608) (76) The white wooden church building still stands on Main Street.

Ira's father Joseph was a Universalist. We do not know Ira's religious preference. It is probable that it was through Ira's sons that the Coles returned to Anglican roots. One influence for this shift might have been his son Charles Lewis' wife, Sarah Almira (Woodruff) Cole. She was of more recent English decent and most likely of the Church of England (Anglican-Episcopal). Another son, Samuel Bailey Cole, is recorded in local histories as having been "a loyal devoted member of the Methodist Episcopal Church." (73) A third son, George Frost, lived and farmed in Beaver Dams until his death in 1884, and was the preacher-in-charge of the Methodist Episcopal parish (1877-1879). (76)

Our progenitor, Ira's son Charles Lewis Cole, had no known church affiliation, but his son Ira was the senior warden at St. James Episcopal Church in Watkins for 20 years. (73) Charles' other son, Frank, was a devout Episcopalian much involved in church activities in nearby Elmira. His son, Stuart Gottlieb Cole became a priest of the Episcopal Church in 1928. Coles in this line have remained communicants in the Episcopal Church in America.

Ira and his family began their new life as farmers in the area when he was only 26 years old. Through hard work he built a profitable cash-crop business and purchased additional land. The Coles eventually owned most of the land from Chambers to Beaver Dams. Local records show:

"Ira and Nancy (Bailey) Cole were farming people living in the town of Catlin, where they settled in the year 1830. Upon the farm . . . but one acre of land had been cleared and upon it stood a log house and a frame barn. With characteristic energy he began its further development and improvement, cleared the tract of land and placed it under a high state of cultivation, making it a good farming property." (73)

Ira found time to be active in community life. He is listed as supervisor for the Town of Catlin from 1837 to 1839, and again in 1855, as well as justice of the peace during the period. (25, p. 325) We know that this was the same Ira Cole who was married to Nancy Bailey, as Asahel Cole's son Ira was not born until 1839. No other Ira Cole is known to be living in the region at the time.

Beaver Dams Area Map Noting Ira and George Frost Cole Farms, 1863

Ira acquired considerable land in the area during his lifetime. His property south of Beaver Dams, along with that of his son and neighbor, George Frost Cole, appear in District 77 of Schuyler County map published in 1863. Ira sold 71 acres in the Town of Catlin in 1876, one year before his death. His son Charles and other family members inherited the original 65-1/2 acres in 1877. (77) Charles sold his rights to the land to his brother Samuel Bailey in April 1880. He was living with his family in Watkins on Seneca Lake.

Nancy lost her sight before her 55th year and died on the family farm on November 16, 1868, at age 61. Ira remarried. Nothing is known of his second wife except that she was considerably younger. Her gravestone reveals her first name was Harriet and her middle initial "E". Ira died in Beaver Dams on March 3, 1877, at age 72. Harriet died in Beaver Dams on March 25, 1889, at age 52. Ira, his father Joseph, Ira's two wives Nancy and Harriet, and his daughter Minerva are all buried in the Beaver Dams cemetery. Ira and Nancy had:

George, b. April 1827; d. June 12, 1827, at age 2 months. Buried in a family plot near Long Pond.

Phebe Ann, b. March 26, 1828; m. Catlin, NY, July 4, 1844, William, b. July 24 at Candor, NY, s. of Harrison and Nancy (Petty) Loomis. He enlisted in Company F., NY State Engineers in 1862 and served during the Civil War. He d. in a hospital in Virginia, September 2, 1864, apparently from war wounds or disease. She d. Post Creek, NY, November 5, 1856.

George Frost, b. April 25, 1829; m. Post Creek, Chemung Co., NY, December 24, 1850, Mary Almira, b. Ulysses, Tompkins Co., NY, May 8, 1825, dau. of Henry and Hepsibah (Van Loom) Stewart. He was a farmer and preacher-in-charge at the Methodist Episcopal Church (1877-79) in Beaver Dams. His farm was south of his father Ira and Uncle Charles Green's property. (77) He d. at Beaver Dams, September 8, 1884. She d. October 19, 1908.

Minerva, b. December 9, 1832, in Beaver Dams as were all the successive children; m. Beaver Dams, August 6, 1850, Thomas K. b. Hornby, NY, July 10, 1828, s. of William and Mary (Mapes) Hurley. She d. Beaver Dams May 30, 1858. There is no date for his death.

Marinda, b. December 9, 1832, twin of the above; m. July 3, 1851, to James L., b. March 9, 1829, at Wayne, NY, s. of John Lion and Mrs. Sarah (Hodge) Schuyler Gardner. He d. Luther, Mich., February 25, 1901. She d. on date unkn., but after 1908, in Clarkstown, MI.

Susan, b. February 8, 1838; m. Horseheads, NY, October 3, 1855, Lovette LaFever, b. Reading, NY, September 8, 1828, s. of Minard and

Margaret (Obert) LaFever. He d. Beaver Dams, August 13, 1894.
She d. Beaver Dams, December 13, 1926.
Charles Lewis, b. March 21, 1842.
Samuel Bailey, b. January 24, 1847, Catlin, NY; d. December 7, 1912,
Townsend, NY. He m. July 23, 1869, Ursula Dean, dau. of Jarvis
and Mary (Miller) Dean of Townsend, Putnam County, NY. The
1893-1994 Schuyler County Business Directory shows he owned an
eight-acre farm and house on Rt. 32. A biographical record published
during the period carries this account:

*"For twenty years Samuel B. Cole has been engaged in general merchandising
in Townsend. He is a self-made man who, starting out in business life
without capital, has steadily worked his way upward and is now numbered
among the men of affluence in his community. Systematic, trustworthy, and
persevering—upon this foundation he has built his prosperity and has awakened
uniform confidence and good will by his integrity and uprightness.*

*"Samuel B. Cole was provided with good educational privileges and at
the age of sixteen he left school to become an active factor in business life and
to provide for his own support through his personal labor. For twelve years
he was connected with farming interests and then with the capital that he
had acquired through his enterprise and economy he embarked in general
merchandising, opening a store in Monterey in 1880. There he remained for
two years and then removed to Townsend where he has since made his home
and conducted a business that has constantly grown in volume and importance
until it has reached quite extensive proportions for a town of the size. He
carried a large stock of general merchandise of all kinds.*

*"Mr. and Mrs. Cole have a pleasant home in Townsend, where their
friends are many and where cordial hospitality is extended them by the best
families of the community. In his political views Mr. Cole is a Democrat and
for sixteen years he has efficiently served as the postmaster of Townsend. He
also filled the office of assessor for two years, and no trust reposed in him has
ever been betrayed in the slightest degree. He is a man of sterling rectitude of
character and of unquestioned probity, and his wife is a loyal and devoted
member of the Methodist Episcopal Church."* (73)

8th Generation

Charles Lewis *(Ira⁷, Joseph, Jr.,⁶ Joseph⁵, Elisha, Jr.,⁴ Elisha³, William²,
Daniel¹)* m. Horseheads, NY, December 13, 1865, Sarah Almira Woodruff,
born Enfield, NY, April 22, 1842, daughter of Dr. Charles Hyde and Elizabeth
(Hunting or Huntington) Woodruff. (73) Charles Hyde Woodruff, born May 28,

1803, was the son of William Woodruff who married July 16, 1795, Prudence ("Pruda") Hyde, born November 2, 1775. She was a descendant of William Hyde, Jr, born 1565 in Denton, Lancashire, England. He was related to Edward Hyde, Earl of Clarendon, whose daughter, Anne, married the future James II of England, and was mother to Queen Mary II and Queen Anne. The Hyde family held considerable land in England. (80)

Charles Lewis Cole was born and raised on the family farm near Beaver Dams. On July 21, 1862, at age 20 he enlisted in the Union Army at Elmira, NY, for a period of three years. His military records show he stood 5'-10", had gray eyes, light hair and fair complexion. His tall, thin frame earned him the nickname "Stovepipe". He might have stated his age as 21 when he enlisted, which is the age shown on his military enlistment records.

The 107th Regiment of the NY Infantry (Volunteers) had been organized at the direction of President Lincoln and granted authority by the War Department only two days before. The President was beset by demands that recruiting be increased after a year of disaster on the battlefield. He called upon Congressmen to direct the organization of volunteer regiments. The New York Representative for the Elmira area was called to meet with the President and agreed to form a new regiment. This presented little difficulty, as "every man, woman, and child seemed to be a recruiting agent and so rapid were the enlistments that (those in charge) had all they could do in attending to the mustering in and organizing of recruits". (26, p. 678) So overwhelming was the response that the regiment was quickly oversubscribed with one thousand and thirty-one officers and enlisted members. The regiment was mustered into Federal Service at Elmira on August 13, 1862, less than a month after Charles enlisted.

Charles entered onto the rolls of his regiment as a Private on July 26, 1862. He was shown as "available for duty" and "mustered in" as part of Company E. He was moved to Washington, arriving there on August 15. Only four weeks after issuing the directive, President Lincoln reviewed the new regiment in the nation's capital, a distinction awarded in consideration of its being the first to respond to the call for 300,000 volunteers. (26, p. 678)

The area across the Potomac in Virginia now occupied by Arlington National Cemetery was a Union army camp in 1862. The property had been the estate of Robert E. Lee until 1861 when, shortly after Lee declined the command of the Union forces, the plantation and Custis-Lee mansion were seized. It is here that Charles Lewis encamped and trained before his first engagement with the enemy. His view of Washington from the western bank of the Potomac was quite different from that of today, as construction on the Washington Monument, begun in 1848, was only partly complete. A 150-foot stone masonry stump was all that existed until construction resumed in 1876. It was not completed until 1885, finally reaching a height of 555 feet.

The regiment joined the XII Corps of the Army of the Potomac and later joined the Army of the Cumberland where it served for the remainder of the war. The 107th New York Infantry participated in more than forty engagements during its career.

Charles remained with Company E of the 107th for the balance of the war. According to oral history, he participated in the major Civil War battles of Antietam Creek, Chancellorsville, and Gettysburg, as well as lesser engagements. These three decisive battles were critical in shaping the outcome of the war.

Considered too inexperienced, the 107th was held in reserve at the Battle of Bull Run and saw its first action at Antietam. The battle at Antietam Creek took place on September 17, 1862, near Sharpsburg, Maryland, less than two months after Charles enlisted. It was the bloodiest battles of the war, with the two sides suffering 23,500 casualties. It was there that General McClellan's Army of the Potomac stopped General Lee's initial thrust into the north.

The 107th suffered no casualties at Fredricksburg, where hundreds of Union soldiers died while assaulting Lee's army on the slopes of Marye's Heights. Three months later at Chancellorsville in Maryland, "the single bloodiest event of the war", they bore the brunt of Stonewall Jackson's charge following a night's march around the flanks of the Union army. "It was an awful struggle for existence . . . and many of our killed and wounded were burned in the woods." (26, p. 679)

The Confederate Army was not the only foe. Forces of both sides recorded thousands of deaths from epidemics caused by inadequate sanitation and limited medical facilities. The period between Antietam in September 1862 and Chancellorsville in May 1863 was marked by more than 100 deaths in the regiment from typhoid, malaria, and similar diseases.

The Union Army, under the command of General Hooker, was defeated by General Lee at Chancellorsville. It was Lee's last great victory. He lost Stonewall Jackson in the engagement. He was killed by a shot from his own forces during the fighting that lasted into the night.

The Battle of Gettysburg was fought July 2-3, 1863. This time the Army of the Potomac under the command of General Meade blunted Lee's second invasion of the north and seized the initiative, which was never again lost. More than 7,000 men died, and 44,000 were wounded or missing in the fierce fighting in the fields around Gettysburg.

The 107th was part of the Twelfth Corps of the Army of the Potomac held in reserve at Gettysburg and was subjected to only light fire as it attended to picket duty and the building of fortifications. The regiment returned to Virginia in August.

In September 1863 the 107th Regiment was sent west and made part of the 20th Army Corps under General Hooker. However, according to his army records Charles was hospitalized starting that month, first briefly in Washington and then at DeCamp USA General Hospital on David's Island in New York harbor. His condition on the company rolls was simply listed as "sick" and absent for duty. Whatever his physical ailment, whether a wound or disease, he apparently recovered steadily and by January 1864 he was well enough to perform duty as a hospital attendant at DeCamp. On April 11, 1864, he was transferred to the general hospital at Bedloe's Island, NY.

He rejoined his unit outside Atlanta on May 1864. Half the regiment was killed or wounded in an engagement on May 25, 1864. (26, p. 681) The remainder moved east with General Sherman and was in the battle at Resaca and Gainesville, GA. Charles' unit also took part in engagements at New Hope Church, May 25, 1864; Pine Knob, June 15; Cuff's Farm, June 22; Kemmison, June 27; Peachtree Creek, July 20; and was at the siege of Atlanta, July 23 to August 24. The 107th was among the first units to enter Atlanta and received guard duty as a reward. (26, p. 681) Charles was in General Sherman's 250-mile March to the Sea through Georgia to Savannah between November 15 and December 10, 1864. He was most certainly a combatant, as he was twice noted as having lost his gun sling.

Sherman next turned his army north and regiment records show Charles was shot through the right breast and taken prisoner at Rockingham, NC, March 8, 1865. His capture is recounted in a letter written by Lieutenant Edwin Weller, also of the 107th New York Infantry, a native of Havana (today, Montour Falls) two miles south of Watkins. Edwin was a member of Company H and chronicles his war experiences in letters to his sweetheart Nettie (Antoinette) Watkins. (57)

Edwin Weller provides a first-hand account of events shared by members of the 107th in his letters to Nettie that became more warm and personal over the months of correspondence. They record a Civil War courtship by mail. First addressing her as "Friend Nett" in August 1862, by wars end Edwin was writing to "My Dear Nettie". He married her soon after his discharge in 1865.

Four days after Charles was shot Edwin wrote from Fayetteville, NC:

> *"We have had quite a number of men taken prisoner by the enemy since leaving Savannah. Some twenty from our Regt., among them was a 2nd Lt. from my company.*
> *Tell Daniel (Tracy) that Charley Cole was wounded and taken prisoner by the enemy on the 8th while out forageing (sic). I send word so he may inform his father, who is one of his customers."* (57, pp. 153-156)

Daniel Tracy was married to Nettie's sister and owned a drapers shop selling items needed for sewing. The impression gained from the letter is that

Charles' parents shopped or traded at the store. It might have been Daniel Tracy who first informed Ira and Nancy Cole of their son's announced capture.

According to oral history, however, the enemy did not capture Charles but instead left him to die from his wounds not far from an old log house at Browning Creek, about 12 miles from Rockingham. His shoes and clothing were taken from him. He was unconscious for over 36 hours. During that time he was nursed and cared for by two women who lived nearby. There was no physician to attend to his wounds. He remained there for about two weeks. He then walked with the help of a Negro to Wilmington, NC, and on to Washington.

The following chronicle describing this experience was set down by his great-grandson, Frank H. Cole in 1939, based upon an oral account provided by Frank G. Cole (Charles Lewis' son) who told this story often, having learned it directly from his father. The details, which follow, never varied.

The story:

Charles was on horseback with a small party of men on a scouting mission near Rockingham, NC, on March 8, 1865, while enroute to Fayetteville, NC, with his company. They entered a fenced in field and were moving across slowly on their horses, trying to pick out a good place to leave on the other side. There were many high split-rail fences down south, and it was hard to get tired mounts to jump them. The normal procedure was for someone to dismount, drop rails, and open a door for the others. They were almost through the field when they spotted an enemy patrol. Evidently the enemy had spotted them first and closed off their escape route. The scouting party made a dash to get back out the opening they used to enter the field. It was a trap. Some of the Rebels had dismounted and crept up to this place, anticipating their withdrawal. Charles was on the right flank as the party galloped for the opening. A Rebel on foot jumped up and shot him point blank (so much so that there were muzzle flash burns). A minie ball raced up through his right side. It passed through completely, somehow not being stopped by a rib, and blew him right out of the saddle. A minie ball was a round bullet used by crude weapons that have no rifling. They were not accurate at long distances, but devastating at close range. The impact alone was brutal, and to get one lodged in your body was almost sure death unless the projectile was removed very quickly. The black powder and nearness of horses made tetanus and infections life threatening even if the initial wound did not prove fatal.

The other men retreated, and seeing Charles blasted out of the saddle at point-blank range, assumed he was a "goner". Even the Rebels thought he was dead. They took his shoes and clothing, leaving him where he fell. His official records indicate he was captured on March 8 and declared missing in action on

March 22. Charles was found in the field by two local women who discovered he had a spark of life left. A black man had started to dig a grave for Charles, but the ladies entreated him to help drag Charles to a poor dirt-floor hut with no windows. There, with no help from a regular doctor or any medicines except herbs, they slowly nursed him back to consciousness. It was many days before he could sit up to take nourishment and many more before he gradually got strong enough to move around and walk. The black man eventually helped him to get as far as Wilmington, NC, cooking for him and often scrounging food from the black communities along the way. The black man turned back at Wilmington where someone there gave Charles used clothes and shoes, which didn't fit until he cut out the toes.

He wrote home from Wilmington that he was still alive and walked on to Washington. Army records confirm he passed north through Union lines on April 6, was removed from missing status on April 18, and again hospitalized. The war was drawing swiftly to a close. General Lee surrendered his Army of Northern Virginia to General Grant at Appomattox Courthouse on April 9. John Wilkes Booth shot President Lincoln on the 14th, but that had no impact on the outcome of the terrible conflict that had divided the nation so grievously. The final Confederate armies surrendered to Union forces during late April and early May 1865, ending four years of bloodshed.

The scene in Washington was one of complete chaos. The city was filled with stragglers, deserters, wounded, and others that had legitimately separated from their units. Charles managed to get "verified" and received a small sum toward his back pay. It was not enough to buy a horse or get a train home. Instead of waiting for more money, which would have taken weeks, Charles started working his way back to Elmira.

Charles had been reported dead to his unit in late March 1865. Word was sent to his family, informing them officially of his death. The family grieved, but Charles' mother, Nancy, assured the rest of the family that there was a mistake. The family could not get her to accept his death, even though the news was reconfirmed. Although she had become totally blind by the time he went off to war, she said she had "seen" (had a vision) that Charles had been shot and hurt, but that kind barefoot ladies had taken care of him. She reported he was much better and eating again.

Nancy continued giving progress reports on Charles to the family. She would not allow any talk of his death in her presence. When she indignantly refused to consent to memorial services, the family humored her and secretly had a church service without her knowledge. She kept on with almost daily reports about Charles. The family was very gentle in humoring her, although it was disconcerting to the others in their grief. She was consistent in her descriptions and was specific about details of her visions. The rest of the family could hardly ignore her, as she was active with household chores despite her *blindness. She described the rude hut with dirt floor and the barefoot ladies. Even more remarkably, she announced one morning at breakfast that "Charles has started home now" and that "a black man helps him and cooks warm food at night".*

Nancy Bailey Cole had never seen a black man, even when she had sight, so this new detail made her "visions" seem more bizarre to the family. They became upset with her when she began leaving a sandwich and a burning candle in the kitchen window of the farmhouse each night. The family worried about the fire hazard and that the food would draw mice. Nancy was furious when she found someone had blown out the candle or filched the sandwich. Even if the candle was relit in the morning, she could not be fooled, as she would feel to see how much had burnt. The family soon found that it was easier to leave the food and candle alone rather than face her wrath. She was aware the others didn't believe her visions, but that didn't shake her faith.

One morning in June 1865, when the family came to breakfast, Nancy kept hushing everybody saying, "Charles is home". They all exchanged knowing looks (fearing she was failing mentally) and humored her, but were not particularly quiet. She insisted until they agreed to look in the spare room on the first floor to quiet her. When they entered they found Charles on the floor, sound asleep and filthy dirty. It was evident he had tried the bed first, as it was grimy too.

They all fell upon Charles in their high excitement. His mother had one terrible moment when she felt his face, because he now had a full beard. This was the only discrepancy in the visions she had reported over the past three months. She had even pictured his open-toed shoes correctly, but had always visualized Charles as clean-shaven, as he had been when he went off to war.

The first of his letters saying he was alive and on his way was delivered three weeks after he arrived home. It had been recopied and was in another's handwriting. Evidently, the original had gotten wet and almost illegible. Someone had painstakingly copied it, including the mistakes in spelling. (62)

Charles was "mustered out" and paid $25 of the $100 in back pay owed to him on June 5, 1865, near Washington. After that he began the trip home to the Watkins area, finally arriving by train. He was dropped from his regiment's rolls and discharged in Elmira on June 19. He was owed nearly a years back pay and $11.36 in overdue clothing allowance.

Charles married Sarah Almira Woodruff on December 13, 1865. There are clear indications that Sarah and Charles knew each other well before he enlisted in July 1862. Like Charles, she would have been age 20 in 1862. According to oral histories his family informed Sarah of Charles' death after receiving word in March 1865. In June she traveled to Horseheads with friends to view a train bearing veterans returning from the war. Sarah saw Charles standing on the rear platform of the train as it paused before proceeding to its scheduled stop in Elmira. She fainted on the spot. (67)

He had worked as a farmer on land owned by his father before the war and returned to this work for several years after his return. He and Sarah moved to Watkins sometime before 1877. The Schuyler County Business Directory for 1893-94 lists him as a house and sign painter, and decorator living in the Village of Watkins. He may also have been a furniture maker, as a drop-leaf table and other pieces of furniture ascribed to him remain in the family. The Directory indicates he lived at #6 Second Street. His son, Ira Woodruff, had not yet married and was living with him. Charles' wife Sarah is listed as owning the house and 20+ acres in Dix and Catlin.

The census of 1900 records him as living with Sarah, their daughter Florence (Cole) Colegrove, their granddaughter Olive, "and family". Charles is listed as owning the home, being able to read and write, and occupied as a house painter.

Over the years the family owned at least three homes in Watkins at 6 Second Street (no longer standing); on the corner of Sixth and Franklin Streets (the site of the present post office in Watkins Glen); and 115 Seventh Street (still standing). Sarah eventually converted the Seventh Street home into a boardinghouse, more likely out of compassion than financial need. For a period their daughter Florence, a practical nurse, lived there also no doubt serving the needs of the boarders.

The death certificate records Sarah died in the family home at 115 Seventh Street on Friday January 26, 1911, at age 69. She was much loved in the community and involved in the work of the church. The funeral, held in the family home at 2:00 p.m. the following Monday, was conducted by her pastor, Rev. F.W. Session of the Watkins Methodist Episcopal Church, assisted by Rev. A.W. Ebersole of St. James Episcopal Church and a Rev. McKnight of Elmira.

An obituary in the local paper notes she had been in poor heath but her condition did not become serious until the Christmas season. It also reports:

> *"Mrs. Cole was a lady of sweet and lovable disposition, a kind neighbor, a devoted wife and mother, and a consistent Christian. Her warmth of heart and sympathetic nature endeared her to all with whom she came in contact and won for her the affectionate regard of old and young alike. She ministered with willing hands to the wants of the sick and needy, and the sunshine of her presence brought comfort into many a sorrowing heart. Her death brings sorrow not only to the members of her family, but to the wide circle of friends and neighbors who also mourn the loss."*

Charles lived on in the home until January 6, 1919, when he was placed in the psychiatric hospital in Willard, NY, by his daughter Florence Colegrove. Florence had cared for him after Sarah's death, but had to institutionalize him because he began "wandering away at night." His file at the Willard Psychiatric Center has since been destroyed and is not available for review. We do know from what records remain that Charles died while a patient there on February 4, 1919, less than a month after being admitted. He was 76 at the time of his death. He was diagnosed as suffering from acute cerebral arteriosclerosis. There were apparently no physiological or psychological issues of a genetic nature that should concern his descendants. He simply succumbed to problems common in old age. (73)

Both Charles and Sarah are buried in Glenwood Cemetery in Watkins Glen (the city name was changed from Watkins to Watkins Glen on March 10, 1926). They rest on a tree-shrouded hillside high above Seneca Lake. Charles Lewis Cole and Sarah Almira Cole are pictured on the cover dust jacket (see caption on page 80). Charles and Sarah had three children b. at Watkins, NY:

> **Frank Gerry**, b. November 16, 1866.
>
> Florence Elizabeth, b. October 22, 1871; m. (1) Elmira, NY, January 16, 1888, Walter, b. 1870 in Burdett, NY, s. of Silas C. and Mary E. (Wood) Colegrove. They had three dau.: Katherine Nivison, Mary Wood and Olive Cole Colegrove. She m. (2) Watkins, NY, January 13, 1906, Edward Clarence, b. Elizabethville, PA, September 19, 1874, s. of William and Mary (Martin) Cooper. They lived in Watkins and had two dau.: Marian Sara and Janice Hunting Cooper. He d. November 13, 1941. She d. May 22, 1955, and is buried in Glenwood Cemetery.
>
> Ira Woodruff, b. June 22, 1873; m. at Watkins, NY, October 26, 1898, Fannie Ames, b. there July 28, 1875, dau. of John Spafford and Sarah (Ames) Budd. Ira lived in Watkins, NY, and was a druggist. He left school at age 17 and worked in a local drug store. Upon the death of the owner, Ira bought the business and founded Cole & Son Pharmacy in Watkins. He managed the pharmacy with his s. Frank Ames. Ira most likely interested and trained his brother Frank in the skills of the trade. Ira was Senior Warden at St. James Episcopal Church for 20 years. He d. at his home on Decatur Street, January 23, 1947, at age 72. Fannie d. March 10, 1956.

9th Generation

Frank Gerry *(Charles[8], Ira[7], Joseph, Jr.,[6] Joseph[5], Elisha, Jr.,[4] Elisha[3], William[2], Daniel[1])* m. Horseheads, NY, June 3, 1891, **Rose Belle**, b. May 17,

1871, dau. of Johann Gottlieb and Cornelia (Theurer) Kimmich, Johann's second wife. The marriage took place in the Kimmich home.

Rose Belle (Kimmich) Cole

Rose was born in Horseheads. Her father, Johann Gottlieb Kimmich, emigrated from Kimmichsweiler (Kimmich's hamlet), Württemberg, Germany, in 1860. Kimmichsweiler is a small village near Hegensberg east of Esslingen am Necker, south of Stuttgart in Baden-Württemberg.

Kimmichsweiler began as a small settlement "started in 1750 by J.G. Kimmich, a citizen of Oberesslingen." The initials J.G. probably stood for Johann Gottlieb, as a search of hamlet records shows these forenames were commonly used in each succeeding generation. The Johann Gottlieb Kimmich who emigrated to North America was a direct descendant of the founder of the hamlet. (72)

The Kimmich home at #1 Kimmichsweilerweg (later redesignated # 9 and now # 37) was built in 1779 by Johann Gottlieb Kimmich, grandfather to the Johann Gottlieb who emigrated to the United States. Local records reflect: "J.G. Kimmich built a lodging with families Scheuer, Stallung, and Keller all under one roof, near Oberhof above the vineyard hills". (34, p. 79) It was the family home when Rose's father Johann Gottlieb Kimmich was born there in 1843. It remained a Kimmich residence until 1899.

Johann Gottlieb was born January 6, 1843, and christened January 8 in Evangelisch, Oberesslingen, Neckarkreis, Württemberg. The Baptismal name "Gottlieb" appears frequently in this line of the family. It is derived by combining the two German words (God: Gott and love: lieben) to form "God's love."

His parents were Johann Gottlieb Kimmich (b. January 11, 1791) and Katherina Magdalena Münzenmaier (b. March 6, 1804), daughter of Eberhard Friederick Münzenmaier, a farmer, and his wife Magdalena Dorethea (Traub). Johann and Katherina Münzenmaier were neighbors before they married in 1821, as Friedrich Münzenmaier built his home only two doors away from the Kimmich residence in 1819. (34, p 72).

His grandparents were Georg Friedrich/Friderich Kimmich (b. September 5, 1752) and Maria Margaretha Flaig (b. April 21, 1752) who married February 11, 1777. The Kimmichs had strong ties to the Lutheran Church and records copied from the Evangelische Kirche Oberesslingen proved of great assistance in researching the family. (78) They contain an interesting entry concerning the grandparents:

"11 Feb. 1777 were married the fornicators in the prayer hour Georg Friedrich Kimmich a wine gardener, son of Johannes Kimmich a citizen and wine gardener here (Kimmichsweiler) with Maria Margaretha, daughter of

Hanss Jerg (Johann Georg) Flaig, a citizen and weaver from Köngen, at the time keeper of the estate Kielmann. Note: After the young Kimmich received permission because he was a minor he was allowed to be married. Marriage in Oberesslingen." (69)

This mention of his status as "a minor" is unrelated to his age; as Georg and Maria would have been 24 at the time. The pastor seemed to be particularly vicious in recording information on couples that had sex before marriage. This entry may indicate they had to get married because she was pregnant at the time, and the pastor disapproved.

His great-grandparents were Johannes Kimmich (b. February 27, 1729, d. December 12, 1807) and Rosina Katharina Spieth (b. January 16, 1730, d. January 11, 1800) who m. November 16, 1751. (69) (78) He was the "J.G. Kimmich" who established the settlement in 1750.

Johann Gottlieb's parents Johann and Katherina had 12 children (5 male, 6 female, 1 unkn.). He was the ninth. He and an older brother Karl/Carl Friderich (b. October 10, 1825, d. December 30, 1898) would later emigrate to the United States, following behind their sister, Luise Rosina (b. October 2, 1832, d. July 26, 1909). She reportedly emigrated as early as 1854, at which time she would have been only 22. She applied officially for permanent immigration into the United States in a document signed in Elmira, NY, on July 9, 1863, using the name "Rosine Louise", apparently an anglicized version of her German name. (69)

It is doubtful Rosine Louise would have traveled to the United States alone, and it is clear Johann did not travel with her. While she might have accompanied an uncle or other near relative, it remains to be discovered who sponsored her, who was with her on the journey, and why she settled in the Elmira area. Johann followed his sister, perhaps sponsored by her husband. He traveled to the Elmira area in 1860 when he was just 17. Their brother Karl sailed from Antwerp with his family in the summer of 1865.

Farming was the principal occupation in the Kimmichsweiler. The major crops being sugar beets, mustard seed, and grapes for use in making wine. Municipal records of Hegensberg contains this entry dated October 29, 1868:

"Johann Gottlieb Kimmich (now living in North America), an unmarried baker from Kimmichsweiler, b. January 6, 1843, son of the deceased vintner Johann Gottlieb Kimmich and his deceased wife Katharina Magdalena (Münzenmaier) Kimmich, has formally applied for (1) a permanent permit to emigrate and (2) to settle his financial holdings, judged to be worth approximately 1,100 'Gluden'. Since he has agreed to renounce his Hegensberger citizenship rights for the State of Württemberg, and Christian Friedrich Bühler vouches for him, both requests are granted." (72)

The date January 6, 1843, corresponds with Cole family records and clearly establishes this to be the Johann Gottlieb Kimmich whose daughter Rose married Frank Gerry Cole.

While little is known of the family other than they were vintners, local records reflect that Johann's great-grandfather was an "attorney" for the community of Oberesslingen from 1750 to approximately 1790. This was an honorary, appointed position. The attorney was a deputy of the public defender for citizens in the hamlet. He "worked for Schultheiss of the Oberesslingen district and was obligated to the community of Hegensberg to maintain law and order. He was a member of the community's citizens' council, and the judge for orphans, and belonged to the church council." (34, p. 132). The reference is confirmation that the Kimmichs were not only prospering as landowners but also prominent in community life and entrusted to hold positions of authority.

The name "Kimmich" is not exclusive to the Kimmichsweiler area. It is found throughout Württemberg and many by that name emigrated to North America and Africa beginning early in the 19th Century. Nearly four million Germans came to the United States between 1850 and 1893. Emigration was spurred by a variety of factors, including crop failures in Europe, lack of industrial employment, over population, social discontent, political repression, and a desire to avoid military conscription. There was also the lure of cheap land and the chance to make a fresh start in a new country.

There were two main German ports of embarkation (Bremen and Hamburg) where German officials prepared detailed lists of all emigrants. The lists have since been carefully collected and reproduced. (22) The New York customs office recorded all passenger arrivals from 1820 through June 17, 1897, but these lists have not yet been indexed. The Center for Immigration Research has considered undertaking the task. (55)

The census of 1910 confirms Johann arrived in the United States in 1860, but no record has been found showing his departure point, port of entry, or departure/arrival dates. As his name does not appear in the very complete records kept by German port authorities at Bremen and Hamburg, it is probable he traveled through France or Holland and booked passage from Le Havre, Antwerp or Rotterdam. These coastal cities were also major departure points for individuals and families seeking a better life across the Atlantic. Authorities at these ports were not as efficient as the Germans in keeping records of such events.

Johann Gottlieb Kimmich likely arrived at Castle Garden in New York harbor. The island was surrounded by a 13-foot-high fence to keep out unscrupulous agents. Here newcomers would register, be examined, eat, bathe and arrange for lodging or transportation for themselves and their luggage before proceeding into the city via a landfill bridge. The most famous New York embarkation point, Ellis Island, was not put into use until 1892.

Sailing ships of the day were masted vessels of various sizes. They were often overcrowded and lacked adequate toilet facilities. This contributed to the outbreak of disease and earned them the title "coffin ships."

Johann's brother Karl married Karolina/Caroline Friedericke Mattes (b. August 27, 1832) on July 31, 1853, and their first child, Maria Carolina, was born five months later on December 26, 1853. Family letters report that as a young girl, Caroline Mattes was "picked up in France during a war between France and Germany, and taken into Germany (to be) with a family in Kimmichsweiler to be kept until he (her father?) came back for her". He never returned after the war. (69)

Karl applied for emigration to the United States on June 30, 1865, and his application was approved. Ship records confirm that the "wine dresser Carl-Friedr. Kimmich" boarded the ship J.F. Chapman in Antwerp on September 20, 1865, with his wife and six children (two boys, four girls), the youngest six months and the oldest six years. (22, Vol. 16, p. 339)

The young family had a tragic crossing. Caroline and both the oldest and youngest of the children (Maria Carolina age 8 and Frederick Pauline 6 mo.) died of cholera or typhoid fever on the 90-day journey, prolonged by the on-board epidemic that prevented the ship from docking in New York. The manifest lists all the names as if to imply they arrived safely, but family records indicate the three died at sea. (69) Most manifests at the time simply listed those who boarded and paid passage, not those who arrived safely. Only Karl, daughters Rosina Catharina "Kate" (age 7), Caroline Regina "Carrie" (6), and Louise Regina (4), and his son Carl Gottlieb (3) survived the journey.

Karl's family was soon to endure additional pain. His son, little "Gottlieblie", drowned in the stream running through Elmira. According to a family letter:

"Gottlieblie, Mommie always called him. The poor little fellow drowned in a stream in Elmira while washing his feet. He was never allowed to go home until he washed his feet in the stream, and a neighbor from her upstairs window saw him drown; screamed out of her window for help, but too late." (69)

Johann had been living in Elmira with or near his sister Rosine Louise for five years when Karl arrived. Johann was most likely working as a baker in Elmira before opening his own business in the nearby community of Horseheads. Horseheads got its name from sun-bleached horse skulls found there years after General Sullivan's army mercifully killed exhausted packhorses during its 1779 campaign against the Iroquois Indians. German records confirm Johann was a "Bäckermeister" (master baker) before emigrating and oral histories establish he was a baker at the Civil War prison camp built in Elmira in 1864.

Elmira became a center for the mustering and dispatching of Union soldiers after the Civil War erupted in 1861. Officers were sent there to train the men and Elmira became one of three military depots in the state, the others being at Albany and New York City. Three large army camps, two hospitals, and a vast storehouse for supplies were built. Before these were finished, churches, warehouses, public halls, and business buildings of various kinds were pressed into service.

In the early part of 1864, one of the three Union camps in Elmira was nearly empty. The government decided to use it as a prison camp for captured Confederate soldiers. The camp was on Water Street above Hoffman Street. (54, p. 35)

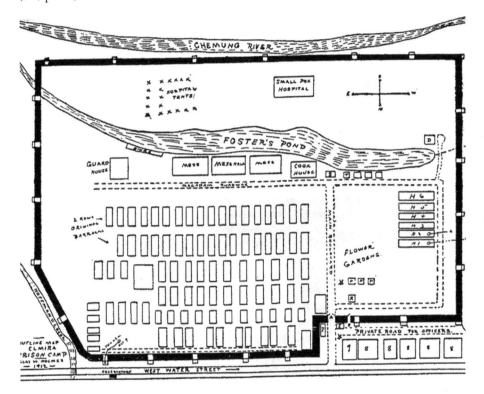

Elmira Prison Camp, 1865

Main Entrance at lower right near officers' homes; mess and cook houses at upper center near Foster's Pond; barracks in center; and hospital tents and small pox hospital at top.

A 12-foot wood fence surrounded the camp with a walk for sentinels on the outside three feet below the top, providing a clear view of movement within. The barracks could hold 4,000 prisoners and there was room in tents for another 1,000.

The first order to move prisoners to Elmira was dated June 30, 1864. It instructed the commander of Point Lookout on Chesapeake Bay to forward 2,000 enlisted prisoners to Elmira. The first prisoners arrived by train on July 6. Forty-five days later there were 9,619 prisoners in the camp designed for 5,000. The 35 buildings were full and half the prisoners were housed in tents. (12, pp. 1279-1286).

In his book, *The Boys' War*, Jim Murphy wrote: "The worst Union prison camp was in Elmira, NY, and contained ninety-six hundred prisoners inside a forty-acre enclosure". (36, p. 82) This statement is disputed, however, in Clayton Wood Holmes' very extensive review, *The Elmira Prison Camp: A History of the Military Prison at Elmira, New York, July 6, 1864, to July 10, 1865.* (27) He details the daily ration prisoners received, noting the issuance of their daily bread, likely baked by Johann Kimmich. There was apparently plenty of bread, but a shortage of vegetables and meat. Clean drinking water was abundant. As an illustration of public sentiment and general expression of the citizens of the city, the following editorial was published in the Elmira <u>Advertiser</u> of December 2nd, 1864:

> "The prisoners of war, now confined to Barracks No. 3 in this city, have, from the first, been treated with all the care and consideration that such persons are entitled to receive from Christian nations in any part of the world. The bread, which we have examined, is as good as can be found in any bakery in the city. They receive one pound of fresh meat per day. Onions, potatoes, and other vegetables are provided three times a week. The hospitals are provided with everything used in the hospitals for our own soldiers. The camp is thoroughly policed and cleaned every day. We think homesickness is the prevailing disease. The only real hardship the Confederate prisoners in the Elmira prison camp have to endure is absence from home and confinement."

Major Hannibal D. Norton, 32d, Massachusetts Infantry, was assigned to Elmira in February 1865. He served as the Adjutant General of the Provisional Brigade responsible for guard duty at the prison camp. He writes about the meals:

> "I sampled them every day, and they were good enough for anybody to eat. One time a committee of six Southern governors visited the camp by permission of the President. When showing them around I took them to the cookhouse, and they sampled the bread and soup, and all united in pronouncing them fine. One said, 'better than we get down home'.
>
> "During my life in the South after the war I met scores of men who had been prisoners at Elmira and was heartily greeted by them and commended for the humane treatment accorded them. All over the South I have met them and was always greeted warmly and told that I 'treated them white when they were in Elmira.

"It makes my blood boil when I contrast our treatment of the Confederate prisoners at Elmira with that accorded our men at Libby, Belle Isle, Salisbury and Andersonville. The death rate at Elmira (nearly one in four) is easily understood when one considers that when the prisoners came to Elmira they were in most instances wasted by disease, hunger, and exposure, and of course unable to withstand the rigors of the northern climate." (27, pp. 88-93, 271-272)

While no record of Johann's activities within the camp has been located, some perspective of the environment he worked in can be gained from reading Holmes' book. Holmes makes no specific mention of the individual cooks and bakers, but notes that a Union sergeant was in charge and confederate prisoners directed the most routine activities of the "cookhouse" staff working in the camp. The cookhouse was located within the confines of the camp not far from the barracks. Five cook ovens for making bread daily were next to the cookhouse. They were made of brick, built square, and held together by iron rods. Each had a capacity of 1,000 loaves a day. (27, pp. 344-345) Many cooks were prisoners and they earned the enmity of their fellow confederates for stealing extra portions. Oral histories indicate Johann was reprimanded often for making the food he prepared "too good" and for asking for more prisoner helpers than needed in order to help the men survive.

Three prisoner mess halls were next to the cookhouse. The sergeants' and officers' mess halls were outside the compound, as was the commissary storehouse. The commissary and cookhouse staffs were undoubtedly busy from before dawn until dusk preparing meals for the camp staff and prisoners. The Elmira camp housed and fed more than 12,000 prisoners between July 1864 and the transfer of the final 140 to a U.S. General Hospital on July 10, 1865. (27, p. 260)

Johann continued to ply his trade at a baker after the war. The Elmira City Directory of 1884-1885 lists him as a baker still living there. (73) He married (1) Anna Boetiker in 1867. They had one son, Robert John Kimmich, born February 16, 1868. Anna died 13 days later on February 29, 1868, from complications at the time of the birth. This accounts for Johann being listed as unmarried in the records of Hegensberg in October 1868. Census records show he was a boarder at 13 Magee Street for a time following Anna's death. He married (2) January 10, 1870, Cornelia Matilda Theurer, born April 9, 1853, also a native of Germany. He was 27. She was 16. He had been widowed for nearly two years by this time, and his young son needed a mother.

Johann's sister Rosine Louise (Luise Rosina) married (1) Noah Theurer. Their first child, Cornelia, was born 1853 according to the census of 1865. Noah d. in November 1865 and Rosine married (2) George Fager who adopted her five children, including Cornelia. This is confirmed in George Fager's obituary published in the Elmira Star Gazette on December 23, 1911. It states he was survived by a stepdaughter "Mrs. J. G. Kimmick (Cornelia)" living in Horseheads. Cornelia was therefore Johann's niece as well as his wife. (68)

Cornelia was stepmother to Robert John and also gave birth to Rose Belle (b. May 17, 1871, d. February 22, 1957), Emma Louise (b. March 21, 1873, d. December 15, 1962), Amelia "Mille" Cornelia (b. February 6, 1875, d. unkn., but after 1973), Katherine Grace. (b. July 18, 1877, d. May 14, 1963), Anna May (b. March 15, 1880, d. December 27, 1881—mysteriously, her headstone reads "1881-1883"), and one son Frederick Gottlieb (b. March 26, 1884, d. December 21, 1905).(69) Tragically, Frederick, who was to be their only son, died at age 21. An obituary in the Elmira Gazette and Free Press reported on December 21, 1905:

> *"Frederick Kimmich of Horseheads died this morning at 10 o'clock at Colgate University in Hamilton of typhoid pneumonia after a brief illness. Deceased was 21 years of age and one of the most popular young men in the college as attested by his election as captain of the baseball team last fall. He was in his third year and would have graduated in the summer. He is survived by parents, four sisters and one brother: Robert J. Kimmich (NYC), sisters: Mrs. F.G. Cole of Elmira, Mr. H.H. McQueen, Mrs. Rho L. Bush, and Katharine Kimmich of Horseheads."*

The Kimmich family lived in Elmira at 621 Lake Street in 1884, 418 Madison Avenue in 1885, and 663 Lake Street in 1886. (68) Johann and Cornelia settled in nearby Horseheads by 1887 where they opened a bakery on Hanover Square and lived out their lives. Johann appears to have anglicized the spelling of his family name to correspond with its common pronunciation. His business stationery carried the following return address: J.G. Kimmick, Baker, Grocer, Confectioner, Horseheads, NY. The bakery was located at 59 North Main Street, a three-story building with the shop at street level and apartments above where the family lived initially.

The "Kimmick (sic) Bakery" sold a square loaf of bread "for a nickel". A team of gray horses pulled a delivery wagon as far as Elmira making daily deliveries. (11, p. 176) Johann was a religious man known as having a soft heart for the needy and hungry. He was notorious for providing support and free baked goods to other German immigrants, particularly those from the Württemberg area.

Johann was 67 at the time of the 1910 census, had become a naturalized citizen by this time and had been married to Cornelia for 40 years. He was listed as the proprietor of the family bakery in Horseheads where Cornelia was listed as being employed as a baker and "assistant proprietor". The census document shows a 27-year-old white "servant" Henry Baker was living in a family home at 121 N. Main Street, along with a second boarder, Ruth Elston, age 20 who was shown as "attending school any time since September 1, 1909." The Kimmichs owned the home free from any mortgage.

Johann died at home near noon on September 4, 1921, at age 78. He is buried in the Maple Grove Cemetery in Horseheads. His headstone bears the Anglicized spelling of his name: John G. Kimmick. Cornelia died June 14, 1931, at age 78, and is buried next to him, as are three of their children: Anna May, Frederick Gottlieb and Katherine. The family name on all their gravestones is the Anglicized spelling: Kimmick.

Frank Gerry Cole

Charles Lewis Cole's son Frank married Rose Kimmick in 1891 when he was 25 and she was 20. Frank was athletic as a young man and, according to one story, skated the 22-mile length of Seneca Lake from Watkins to Geneva on one of the rare days the lake was frozen. He was an apprentice pharmacist in Watkins in 1881 and worked in drug stores in Syracuse, NY, and Sayre, PA, before moving to Elmira with Rose and their children, Ira, Ruth and Charles in 1897. There were few "patent" medicines at that point in history and drug stores either furnished the raw materials or pharmacists compounded cough syrups, fluidextracts, tinctures, and elixirs to be dispensed on prescription.

The Cole family was numerous and widespread in central New York at the time. A newspaper account of the 37th Cole family reunion held at the home of Harvey F. Cole in Dryden noted 83 members attended, including "Mr. and Mrs. Frank G. Cole, Ruth Cole, and Mrs. J.G. Kimmick (sic) of Elmira." (62)

Oral history relates that Frank was asked by the British Crown to sign a release of property rights on land held in England. This happened sometime between 1932 and 1939. The reference is very vague, but it would imply that this branch of the family might have held title to property in England. The most probable connection is the lineage through his great-grandparents, William and Prudence (Hyde) Woodruff, and the Hyde family in England.

Frank and Rose raised their children in the family home at 405 Perry Street (census of 1900), 457 E. 2nd Street (census of 1905), and 220 William Street (census of 1910) in Elmira. He was active in community and church life, and a vestryman at Trinity Episcopal Church. He was a pharmacist for 58 years, 42 of them in Elmira, and was a partner and active head of the Terbell-Calkins Drug Company, a Rexall Drug Store at 323 E. Water Street when he died November 1, 1939, at age 72.

His obituary that day stated he had been ill for two weeks, but went to work at the drug store on Tuesday afternoon. He arose on Wednesday to go to work and was stricken with a fatal heart attack in his home at 220 William Street. The time of death is listed as 8:15 a.m. and the cause as acute coronary thrombosis. According to oral history, he was listening to the radio, bent forward to tie his shoes, leaned back in his chair, and expired.

The Round Town column in the local paper mourned the loss to the community. Its writer, Matt Richardson, noted:

> "It was a sad blow, indeed. Few men have been identified with one business concern for so many years, and not many have succeeded in making so many friends. He was painstaking; courteous . . . and any concern fortunate enough to have a man possessing loyalty and personality sufficient to retain old patrons and attract new ones has an asset to be guarded carefully . . . Elmira will miss Mr. Cole."

Rose and her two unmarried adult children, Charles and Ruth, soon moved to 312 W. Gray Street, where Rose died February 22, 1957, at age 85. According to her death certificate she fractured her hip in a fall at home three days earlier and was in a coma for 48 hours immediately before her death. She was a jovial, short, heavyset woman who was much loved by family and friends. Her molasses cookie recipe remains in the family and is a favorite, particularly among the children.

The Cole family home at 312 W. Gray Street still stands and has been designated a National Historic Site, one of the landmark homes in Elmira's Near Westside Historic District. Frank and Rose are buried near the Kimmich family at Maple Grove Cemetery in Horseheads. Frank and Rose had:

Ira Earl, b. Syracuse, NY, March 15, 1892. He graduated from Elmira Free Academy and Cornell University (1915) with a degree in Mechanical Engineering. He worked on submarine detection projects for the National Research Council during World War I. Ira m. June 3, 1925, Anna Hermann from Richmond Hill, Long Island, NY, a graduate of Barnard College. Together they had: Catherine Irene (b. August 3, 1926), Frank Hermann (b. September 26, 1929, d. October 21, 2005), and Rosemarie (b. February 15, 1931). Ira was a transmission research specialist with Bell Telephone Laboratories in Montclair, NJ, for most of his professional career. During World War II, he was in charge of developing a printing telegraph system for transatlantic radio use. He retired in 1957 after 32 years with the company and joined the Lockheed Electronics Company in Plainfield, NJ, in 1960 as a senior electronics engineer. Ira was the holder of 11 patents. He d. October 21, 1968, at age 76 from injuries sustained in an automobile accident 10 days earlier.

Ruth Matilda, b. Syracuse, NY, May 18, 1894. She was a graduate of Elmira Free Academy and Elmira College. She did not marry, saying she "never found the right man at the right time." Ruth devoted her life to teaching social studies and commercial business at Southside High School in Elmira, a position she held for 40 years until retirement in 1961. She was an active member of Grace Episcopal Church where she served on the Altar Guild for many years. She d. April 27, 1987, at age 92.

Charles Frederick, b. Cross Forks, PA, March 12, 1896. He attended Elmira Free Academy, but left one month before graduation. He served with the American Expeditionary Force in France during World War I as part of Company H, 21st Engineers, composed largely of men from Elmira with experience working on the Lackawanna Railroad. Company H was the first to run a steam engine with supplies up Mount Sect near Verdun under heavy German artillery fire after a major allied drive in the region, just prior to the end of the war. General Pershing noted after the war that the work of the railroad and civil engineers was critical to getting supplies to the main forces "against battering assaults from the enemy." Following the Armistice, Charles was assigned to help repair the railroad line between Verdun and Metz, and then sent to Conflanes, Lorraine, to help run the railroad center there until his return to the United States. He never married, having lost the first woman he loved to another man while he was serving in the war. He worked for the railroads for several years after returning home and then joined his father preparing prescriptions in the drug store. While not a licensed pharmacist, he was particularly skilled in this work. He was admitted to the Bath Veterans Hospital, Bath, NY, on April 23, 1964, at age 68. He suffered from hypertensive cardiovascular disease and left-side hemiplegia that caused him to be mentally confused. He d. there on May 4, 1964.

Stuart Gottlieb, b. Elmira, NY, November 21, 1902.

Cole Family Gathering (1908)

Charles Lewis (age 66) and Sarah Almira Cole (66) (sitting center); Rose Kimmick (37) and Frank Gerry Cole (42) (standing upper left); with their four children, Charles Frederick (12) and Ruth Matilda Cole (14) (standing behind Charles Lewis Cole); Stuart Gottlieb Cole (6) (standing front right); and Ira Earl Cole (16) (standing behind Stuart Gottlieb)

10th Generation

Stuart Gottlieb (Frank^9, Charles^8, Ira^7, Joseph, Jr.,^{6} Joseph^5, Elisha, Jr.,^{4} Elisha^3, William^2, Daniel^1) m. Rochester, NY, July 14, 1930, **Doris Mary Lyons**, b. Lyons, NY, January 17, 1905, dau. of William James and Mary Isabelle (Cullen) Lyons.

Doris Mary (Lyons) Cole

Doris' great-grandfather, Farquahar McCrimmon, was b. in Scotland 1800/1801 and married there Mary MacNeal (b. 1822/23). The McCrimmons and their first daughter, Catherine (b. 1847/48) moved to Glengarry County, Ontario, Canada prior to 1854/55 where their second daughter, Isabelle Mary, was born 1854/55. A third daughter, Sarah, was born 1858. All five members of the McCrimmon family are recorded in the Lochiel, Ontario, census of 1861. The family lived in a log house in the area where Farquahar was a laborer and member of the Free Church (Presbyterian). By 1881 only Farquahar and Mary appear in local records, indicating the three daughters may have married.

Their second daughter Isabelle Mary McCrimmon married (date unknown) Bernard Cullen (Cullenan), a émigré from Ireland. They had eight children. The second, Mary Isabelle, was born February 20, 1879, near Ottawa and would later married William James Lyons. They were to become the parents of Doris Mary (Lyons) Cole who would marry Stuart Gottlieb Cole in 1930 and continue the family line.

The Cullen family moved to Lyons, NY, in Wayne County in 1888. Bernard, a traveling salesman, disappeared while on a business trip and was presumed to have been one of three men who died in a boardinghouse fire that occurred along his route.

Charles Williamson, an Englishman who moved to the area in 1791 to manage the more than two million acre Pulteney estate, formed the village of Lyons in 1797. Williamson had traveled in Europe earlier and visited Lyons (Fr. *Lyon*) in east-central France. The fertile beauty of the west-central region of New York State brought to mind the Saone Valley in France, where Lyons rests at the confluence of the Rhone and Saone rivers. This caused Williamson to select the name Lyons for the new village. (75)

The emigration from Ireland of more than 1.8 million Irishmen in the decade beginning in 1847 was due, in part, to the devastation of a single crop, the potato. The island population had nearly doubled in the years 1800-1840. This, coupled with a steady reduction in the size of individual farm holdings (by 1841, nearly 300,000 farms were under three acres) meant land workers lived hand-to-mouth, feeding their families but producing little excess for sale or storing. The potato was the primary subsistence crop. When a potato blight reached Ireland in the fall of 1846, the effect was devastating. Abundant harvests quickly turned to mounds of putrefying vegetation. Tens of thousands starved. It is likely that both Bernard Cullen and Michael Lyons (b. 1836, d. 1899), who were to become Doris' grandfathers, were motivated to emigrate by both a search for civil peace and the desire to survive.

Irish Catholic farmers were suffering from grinding poverty, insatiable hunger, religious persecution and landlord oppression. Their struggle did not end when they arrived in North America where they were regarded as a distinct and inferior race. In addition to being despised for their Catholic heritage, the industrious nature of the Irish and their willingness to work for low wages presented a threat to those who had arrived earlier. Advertisements for employment frequently carried the admonition: "No Irish Need Apply." The growing number of "famine Irish" created a political and social backlash that enterprising politicians drew upon to stir hate and win elections. In 1854, the anti-Catholic Know-Nothing party won stunning victories running on a platform that attacked Irish Catholic immigrants and called for their deportation.

Michael Lyons had been a teamster according to family records, perhaps from Waterford or County Tyrone, Ireland. (61) Because of his lowly status, it will be difficult or impossible to confirm Michael's county of origin. Besides Waterford or County Tyrone, the Province of Munster (Counties Cork, Limerick, Kerry) in the southwest, and Cornacht (Counties Mayo, Galway) in the west-central part of Ireland are likely candidates, as they contain the largest number of families with Lyons surnames in the registry of 1890.

The Irish Lyons families are distinct from those of the same name found in England, Scotland and France. The name probably originated with 12th Century Normans in the French city of Lyons, some of whom migrated to what is today Ireland. They settled initially in County Meath. The name is also found as an anglicized form of O' Liathain (County Cork & Limerick), O'Laighin, or Lyne, an ancient family that owned much property in County Galway until the end of the 17th Century. The family motto: "Don't Irritate the Lions".

After Michael arrived in the United States, family records indicate that he applied his talent as a teamster, leading mules that pulled barges through the portion of the barge canal that passed near the village of Lyons. (61) The opening of the canal in 1825 brought commerce to the area, known primarily for canning and furniture making. The inspiration of the powerful and patriotic

DeWitt Clinton, the 363-mile canal connected the Hudson Valley with the Great Lakes through a series of locks. It created jobs, opened the region to immigration and trade, and brought prosperity to many villages and townships along the route.

By 1862 the four-foot deep ditch had been widened and deepened to eight feet throughout its length to accommodate larger barges. It was renamed the Erie Canal as it stretched as far west as Erie, PA, where it entered into Lake Ontario, creating an unrestricted trade route from eastern cities to the Great Lakes region. Some small barges were poled alone. A team of mules walking along the canal edge pulled the larger ones. As a teamster, Michael would be responsible for controlling a team of mules moving cargo barges up and down the canal in the Lyons area.

Michael (b. 1836, d. 1899) married (date unkn.) Katherine Conner (b. 1848, d. 1900) who was also a émigré from Ireland. He became a U.S. citizen on October 23, 1868, and the family is listed as living in Lyons in the census of 1870.

Michael and Katherine had one daughter, Margaret (b. 1865, date unknown.) and three sons: John (b. 1868, d. 1892), Thomas (b. 1871, d. 1891), and William James (b. 1880, d. 1955). All except Margaret and William are buried in the Roman Catholic North Main Street Cemetery, Newark Village, in the Town of Arcadia, NY.

William James Lyons married Mary Isabelle Cullen in 1904 in Lyons, NY. Mary and William had five children. Doris Mary (b. January 17, 1905, d. February 4, 1973) was their first child. In 1919 a town clerk and in 1968 a clerk at the hospital certified her birth on that date with the name "Dorris Merle Lyons". Her brother Donald remembered her middle name as being "Merle" (61), but her school transcripts and both her marriage and death certificates identify her as Doris Mary Lyons. The use of "Dorris Merle" may be attributable to the careless preparation of the original birth record.

Their other children were: John Cullen (b. 1906, d. August 31, 1920), Donald William (b. February 14, 1911, d. April 16, 2002), Robert Neil (b. April 21, 1913, d. August 23, 1975), and Janet Isabelle (b. January 16, 1918, living). Doris, Don and John were born in Lyons and christened in the Roman Catholic Church there.

Tragically, their first-born s. John died in a swimming accident at age 14. As a newspaper account at the time explains:

> *"Young Lyons, who was secretary of Troop 51 of the Boy Scouts, with some of his other companions, was walking along the bank of Irondequoit Creek. The water looked so inviting that they decided to have a swim. One boy,*

Stewart Carson, ventured out too far and was drawn by the current into a hole where the depth was way over his head. Young Lyons, sensing the danger to his friend, struck out to his rescue, but also became helpless in the deep water, and both boys were drowned. A double funeral was held from St. Stephen's Episcopal Church in Rochester, Saturday afternoon, September 4th."

William worked for the railroad before becoming a mechanic involved in the manufacture of the Mora Automobile built in nearby Newark, NY, a position he held until 1911. His duties included driving, testing, and readjusting machinery on the cars. The Mora was one of the most advanced and reliable automobiles of the period. First produced in 1906, it was constantly updated and improved. The principal stockholder and founder, Samuel H. Mora, had been head of sales for the Eastman Kodak Company in Rochester, NY, and possessed the marketing skills needed to convince the buying public of the "strenuous reliability" of the Mora. (45)

By 1908 a new factory building had been erected and over 200 men were working three shifts a day, six days a week producing hundreds of cars each year. There were more than 200 automobile manufacturers in the country at the time. Despite the competition and a national economic downturn, the Mora Tourer, a six-cylinder top-of-the-line model, sold well.

In the end, engineering and marketing skills were not enough to sustain the company. Efforts to fill a vast number of standing and expected orders led to over-production in the winter and spring of 1910. An extended rainy season that year lessened demand for the convertible-type cars like the Mora, and when suppliers demanded payment for parts already delivered the company was forced into bankruptcy. It was purchased by Frank Toomey, a Philadelphia businessman, who continued operations until July 1911 when the plant began to close permanently. Remaining automobiles were sold and the workmen released. (45, pp. 5-10)

William Lyons was commended when he left the company in a letter of recommendation stating he was "an exceedingly careful driver, and a thoroughly reliable and rapid workman." The letter was dated October 11, 1911, and signed by the superintendent of the Frank Toomey & Company.

The family relocated to Rochester in 1912 before the birth of Bob and Janet. Both were baptized at St. Stephen's Episcopal Church there. William continued to work as an auto mechanic. He was a slight, moody man who in later years was given to brooding and drinking alone in his room. His wife Mary ("Gonna"), a kind and gentile woman, died September 4, 1951, at age 72. William ("Pop") died April 12, 1955, at age 75. Both are buried in Elmwood Cemetery, Lyons, NY.

Doris Lyons Cole, 1924

Doris Lyons, their first-born child, graduated from West High School in Rochester, NY, June 15, 1923. She received a Teacher Training-Craft Education Certificate in Applied Arts from Bevier Art School, Rochester Athenaeum and Mechanical Institute (today, Rochester Institute of Technology) on June 24, 1926. She was teaching art at Sherrill High School in Sherrill, NY, in 1930 when a young Episcopal priest, Reverend Stuart Cole, accepted an invitation to present the invocation at a class commencement. Doris was in charge of the commencement program. She met him when he arrived by train and a friendship began that ended in their marriage in Rochester seven months later at her family parish, St. Stephen's.

Doris was lighthearted with a good sense of humor, intelligent, well spoken, gracious, and socially charming. She enjoyed entertaining in the early years, a definite asset to Stuart's ministry. Her art background and sense of color contributed to the tasteful appointment of each rectory the family occupied. Stuart left all such decisions to Doris. The result was always a pleasing blend of colorful fabrics and dark-wood antiques purchased at home or farm auctions during the Great Depression. She also expressed her artistic talent through needlepoint, several pieces of which remain in the family. (65)

Stuart and Doris married on July 14, 1930, and had two sons, Stuart Hadley (b. May 24, 1931, d. January 3, 1999) and David Charles (b. September 22, 1936, living). Doris was a comforting mother, nurse, and tutor to her two sons, supplementing their public school studies with lessons at the kitchen table.

Good manners and formal courtesies were important to Doris. She orchestrated a ritual family dinner in the rectory dining room each Sunday soon after the 11:00 a.m. service. Everything was proper: lace tablecloth, placemats, candles, silver rings holding neatly pressed napkins, the fine china (always with a butter plate and butter knife), and the best silverware, always properly aligned. Doris sat at one end, Stuart at the other, with one son on each side completing the family circle. Neither boy left the table without asking for and receiving permission to be excused. The favorite meal after church on Sunday was roast beef with Yorkshire pudding. (65)

These pleasant family gatherings provided an opportunity for all to share the events of the week. When Stuart Hadley, the oldest son, went off to preparatory school out of state and then on to college, the pattern changed. The Sunday dinner, still special for Doris, was more often shared at a local restaurant with David and his father.

Doris enjoyed dining out on other days as well. Such occasions often marked the highlight of her week. It was a special treat when Stuart escorted her to the local country club where they were the dinner guests of a well-to-do parish family. She favored a glass of Sherry before a meal, lettuce section with Roquefort dressing, broiled scallops, and fresh asparagus with a hollandaise sauce—served slowly in an elegant setting. (65)

She always had someone to maintain the rectory yard and gardens, do the wash, and clean the house. During the Depression and World War II there was also a cook and a maid to do the serving. Those were difficult times for most. Stuart and Doris helped out a series of farm girls by providing room, board, and a salary in exchange for such household chores. David even had a nanny for several years that cared for and played with him before he entered school. Doris fired her when David was five because she was "stealing affection" from his mother.

Doris made many sacrifices for the welfare of others during Stuart's ministry and their marriage of 42 years. She settled into a state of mild depression toward the end of her life, brought on in part by her sense of isolation. With the boys grown and Stuart regularly involved with ministering to the problems of others, she spent many hours alone in the rectory. She always enjoyed a glass of wine, and eventually became dependent on it as an escape from loneliness. She lost both appetite and weight. Her eventual addiction to wine and cigarettes decimated her physically, but her mind, sense of humor, and spirit remained keen. (65)

It should be noted here that Coles have proven to be generally a happy group, imbued with a quick wit and a confident demeanor. Starting with Doris' father, some have experienced bouts of biological depression. In Doris case, it surfaced in her mid-forties. Her son, Stuart, displayed symptoms in his early fifties. Her second son, David, was 64 before his first episode. The condition is caused by a chemical imbalance in the brain and is easily controllable through the use of anti-depressants medications. Doris, unfortunately, never received the necessary treatment.

Her health slipped steadily after Stuart retired in 1969. She developed cancer of the jaw and mouth as the result of years of heavy smoking. Doris died February 4, 1973, at age 68. She is buried in Maple Grove Cemetery, Horseheads, NY.

Stuart Gottlieb Cole

Stuart ("Tookie") was born on November 21, 1902, in the family home at 457 E. 2nd Street, in Elmira, NY, where he spent his formative years. The Cole family was active in the life of Trinity Episcopal Church where Stuart was baptized (July 19, 1903), confirmed (May 19, 1918), and served as both a choirboy and acolyte.

Stuart graduated from Elmira Free Academy on June 23, 1921. He entered Hobart College, Geneva, NY, that fall, intent on earning a Bachelor of Science degree and going on to teach biology. He received his BS in 1925 but, instead of pursuing a teaching career, he entered the seminary at Bexley Hall, Kenyon College, Gambier, OH, where he completed studies for a Bachelor of Divinity degree in 1928. Stuart returned to Elmira where he was ordained a Deacon in the Episcopal Church in ceremonies held at Trinity Church on April 11, 1928. He was ordained as a Priest of the Episcopal Church in ceremonies there on November 15 the same year.

Rev. Stuart Cole served as Priest-in-Charge for small rural parishes in Sherrill and nearby Canastota, NY, and, beginning in 1930, as curate at St. Paul's Episcopal Church, Syracuse, NY. He and Doris married on July 14, 1930.

In 1932 he accepted a calling to be the Rector of Trinity Episcopal Church in Seneca Falls, NY. The Anglo-Gothic limestone church, built in 1885, is situated in a bucolic setting on the shore of Van Cleef Lake. One of the best preserved church structures in the state, it is listed on the National Registry of Historic Places and features large Tiffany stained-glass windows in the nave. The history of Trinity Church notes Stuart "was extremely popular and beloved by all" during his years in Seneca Falls.

Reverend Stuart Gottlieb Cole, D.D., STD (1955)

Seneca Falls was the birthplace of the women's rights in the United States. In 1848 the Seneca Falls Women's Rights Convention drew together more than 200 women and 40 men, including abolitionist Frederick Douglas. This gathering is widely considered to be the origin of women's rights movement in this country.

The Cole family doctor during the late 1930s was Dr. C. Anna J. Brown, one of the nation's first woman physicians. She received her medical degree from

Syracuse University in 1897 and established the first hospital in Seneca Falls in 1910. (56, p. 41-42)

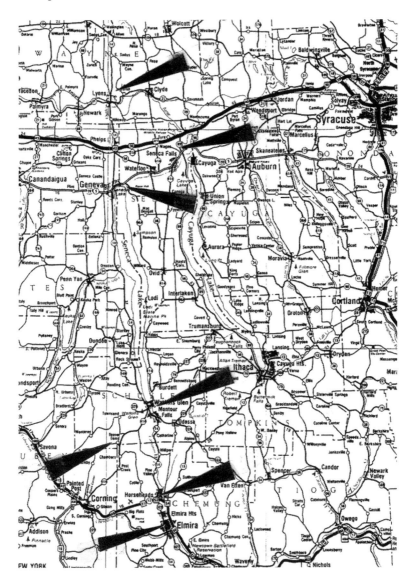

Finger Lakes Region with Family Locations 1830-1949

Stuart was called by the Bishop to leave the parish in Seneca Falls and to move to Geneva in 1939 to serve as Chaplain and Director of Guidance for Hobart and William Smith Colleges. Stuart was also an assistant professor (philosophy and religion), coach of the freshman lacrosse team and, following the outbreak of World War II, Chaplain and counselor for the U.S. Navy V-12 officer-training program on campus.

He returned to parish work as Rector of the Church of the Ascension, Rochester, NY, in December 1944, a position he held until he became Rector of the Church of the Ascension, Lakewood, OH, in the spring of 1949. Both parishes flourished under his ministry and leadership.

He retired from the Lakewood position in 1969 after more than 40 years in the priesthood. The parishioners at the Church of the Ascension pooled resources and purchased Stuart and Doris a retirement home in nearby Bay Village. They remained in the home until her death in 1973. Stuart returned to Elmira to live with his sister Ruth in the family home at 312 W. Gray Street. He moved back to be near friends in the Cleveland area before entering the Episcopal Church Home in Alhambra, CA, in 1985 to be near his two sons and their families living in the Los Angeles area.

Stuart was loved greatly by his many parishioners and colleagues. He was a devout keeper of the faith whose disarming sense of humor put all around him at ease. He devoted his life to others. His work in the church was recognized throughout the Dioceses of New York and Ohio and, in 1954, he was awarded two honorary degrees: Doctor of Sacred Theology (STD) from Hobart College, and Doctor of Divinity (DD) from Kenyon College.

Stuart was a confident, practical person who exhibited excellent business sense when dealing with parish secular issues. He was both a strong spiritual leader and a pragmatic influence on church affairs: he brought souls to Christ while balancing the parish budget. He was renown for the quality of his sermons that were based on the Scriptures yet relevant to the lives of those to whom he preached.

Besides his recognized professional traits, those close to him saw other characteristics commonly found in carefree, fun-loving mortals. Stuart experienced life fully and eagerly, which allowed him to empathize with the worldly problems of those to whom he ministered.

Associates and communicants quickly sensed his confidence, caring way and manifest devotion to God. They were also usually charmed by an infectious sense of humor. Beneath the ecclesiastic veneer coursed playful, impish qualities, and an eternal youthfulness. Doris referred to him as her "Peter Pan".

Stuart was always ready with a joke (often off-color), wore brightly hued clothes (e.g., red plaid sports coat or checkered trousers) when not in clerical black, had a taste for excellent scotch (the finest malts were kept in reserve on a closet shelf), possessed finely tuned card skills (some vestry gatherings were nickel-dime poker smokers in the rectory dining room), enjoyed sports (the National Football League on television, or Sunday morning sandlot baseball while on summer vacation), and was probably happiest with a fishing pole in his hand. (65)

His devotion to the church was constant, however. It was a seven-day-a-week commitment. He was always available to serve those in need and was amused when asked what clerics like he did with their time on the days leading up to Sunday. The phones in the church office and rectory rang at all hours seven days a week as members of his flock called for help with their spiritual needs.

This unceasing demand on his time and energy often interrupted family life and, in later years, strained his relationship with Doris. It eventually became a major chasm in their marriage and, had it not been for the social mores of the time and the nature of his calling, it would surely have led to a divorce.

When death came for Stuart it came quickly and quietly. The floor nurse at the Episcopal Home in Alhambra went to his bed to wake him for breakfast on March 13, 1987, and found him suffering chest pains. She touched Stuart's arm and reassured him she would seek help, but he moved his head from side to side slowly quietly whispered "no". Stuart had lived a full, productive life, and as a Christian he was not afraid of death. Within a very few minutes his heart stopped. He was 84. (65)

A memorial service was held in his family parish, Trinity Church, Elmira, NY, where he had he had been ordained into the priesthood. He is buried in Maple Grove Cemetery, Horseheads, NY, next to Doris, his father Frank, mother Rose, brother Charles, and sister Ruth. A crabapple tree grows between Stuart and Doris' graves, embracing the side-by-side caskets with its roots. Memorial gifts honoring them both can be found in the Hobart and William Smith College St. John's Chapel. A plaque placed there by the colleges reads: "His infinite capacity to share joy, wit, wisdom and love enriched each of God's children whose life he touched". Stuart and Doris had:

> Stuart Hadley, b. May 24, 1931. He married on June 15, 1957, in Long Beach, CA, Pamela Lee, b. April 28, 1933, dau. of Emmett Doster and Evelyn Woodbury (Burpee) Hill of Danbury, CT. Stuart ("Little Tookie") attended public schools in Seneca Falls, Geneva, and Rochester, NY, before entering Williston Academy in Easthampton, MA, graduating in 1950. That fall he entered Kenyon College in Gambier, OH, where he majored in physics. He played varsity soccer and lacrosse all four years and was the captain of both teams in his senior year, when he was also selected to participate in Olympic Soccer Team tryouts in Chicago. Stuart was offered a teaching position in Physics at Williston Academy upon graduating from Kenyon in 1954. Faced with the possibility of being drafted into the U.S. Army, Stuart elected instead to join the U.S. Coast Guard Reserve. He entered Officer Candidate School in New London, CT, and, upon graduation in February 1955, was commissioned Lt. jg. assigned to the USCG Pontchartrain, a weather and rescue vessel stationed in Long Beach, CA. After 18 months he was transferred to

the 13th District Office in Long Beach as a Duty Officer in the Rescue Coordination Center where he received a promotion to Lieutenant. Stuart met Pam in 1956 at All Saints Episcopal Church in Long Beach. She was teaching kindergarten in the public school system at the time. Stuart's father, Reverend Stuart Cole, married them at All Saints in June 1957. They had three children: Stuart Weston (Wes) (b. October 20, 1959); Thomas Sheffield (b. May 4, 1961); and Amy Woodbury (b. August 31, 1962). Stuart separated from active duty in the Coast Guard in December 1957 and joined the Barden Corporation, working in both Los Angeles and Danbury, CT, until 1966. Pam pursued her graduate degree, specializing in teaching preschool deaf and hard of hearing. Stuart joined the Cambridge Institute for Management Education and in 1969 he succumbed to the long-standing urge to teach. He was engaged by Millbrook School in Millbrook, NY, to teach physics and other sciences, and coach several sports. Over five summers he earned his MA degree at Wesleyan University. He became more heavily involved in administrative matters and was ultimately selected to be the Director of Finance at Millbrook School. Pam at the time was teaching at Maplebrook School for "differently-abled" children in Amenia, NY. The family relocated to Japan in 1974 when he accepted a position as the Director of Business Affairs for the American School Japan (ASIJ) near Tokyo. Pam worked as Supervisor of the Junior High Resource Center and taught art history to middle school students at ASIJ. All three Cole children graduated from ASIJ. Returning to the United States in 1987, Stuart and Pam settled in California near their children Wes and Amy, his father Stuart Gottlieb, and brother David. Tom remained in Japan to continue teaching Japanese language at ASIJ. In 1988 Pam was hired as Program Manager for Episcopal Service Alliance (ESA) in nearby Santa Ana, working with the homeless and chemically addicted. Stuart served as Junior and Senior Warden for the local Episcopal parish. Pam later served in the same capacity. Stuart suffered from bouts of depression during the last 25 years of his life, which medication never controlled fully. He also found it increasingly difficult to breath because of the onset of emphysema and, for the last few years of his life, he had to be constantly attached to a portable oxygen supply. Stuart died January 3, 1999, from multiple complications following surgery in mid-November 1998 to remove a benign growth in his lower intestine. Stuart's greatly diminished lung capacity resulting from nearly forty years of smoking contributed to his untimely death. (65)

David Charles Cole, b. September 22, 1936.

11th Generation

David Charles *(Stuart^{10}, Frank^9, Charles^8, Ira^7, Joseph, Jr.,^{6} Joseph^5, Elisha, Jr.,^{4} Elisha^3, William^2, Daniel$^{1)}$* m. May 16, 1964, in Lakewood, OH, **Nancy Carol Murray**, b. November 21, 1942, daughter of Delmar Lee and Lois Evelyn (Taylor) Murray of Arroyo Grande, CA. She was 21 and he was 27. The Cole family experienced an infusion of German/Scottish/Irish and, for the first time, Native American bloodlines.

Nancy Carol (Murray) Cole

Nancy's mother, Lois Evelyn Taylor, born May 24, 1919, in San Bernardino, CA, was the daughter of Walter Ethmer and Cora Elma (Baker) Taylor, and the first child of the second marriage for both.

Cora was the great-great-granddaughter of Johannes Conrad Becker, born in Germany, ca. 1742, a farmer who arrived in Virginia sometime before 1782 when local records indicate he married. As the firstborn son, Johannes returned to Germany with his family to settle his deceased father's estate and collect his inheritance. He reentered the United States in 1797 with his wife and three children and had settled in Greene County, OH, by 1814. The family name was later changed from Becker (meaning baker in German) to Baker. Successive generations continued to farm land in Shelby County, OH.

Cora Elma (Baker) Taylor was born August 2, 1884, daughter of William Webster and Deborah Charlotte (Hartshorn) Baker. She was sent from Sidney, OH, to Kansas at age 12 to live with her grandparents to help with housework and care for her grandmother who was bedridden following a stroke. She married her first husband, Charles Wesley Hayes, at age 16, November 21, 1900, at Princeton, KA. The Hayes family moved to San Bernardino, CA, with their five children in 1913 seeking clean air and relief for Charles' tuberculosis. Charles died there June 12, 1915.

Cora next married Walter Ethmer Taylor, February 5, 1917. Walter was born April 16, 1882, in Perris, AR. He was the son of Christopher Columbus Taylor and Elizabeth (Bell) Taylor of Pine Bluff, AR. Taylor family oral history establishes an ancestral link with President Zachary Taylor and his father, Lt. Colonel Richard Taylor of Orange County, VA, who listed among his forebearers Elder William Brewster of the Mayflower. Confirming this information is left to later researchers.

Walter Taylor was working for Hanford Iron Works in San Bernardino when he married Cora, his first wife Eliza having died without issue. Their first surviving child, Lois Evelyn (Nancy's mother), was born in San Bernardino, May 24, 1919.

Walter and Cora moved to Blythe, CA, in August 1919, after a kitchen fire destroyed their dwelling and belongings. Three-month old Lois was rescued from the burning home when those outside suddenly realized they had fled without her. The Taylors settled in a shack house in Blythe with their six children, five from Cora's first marriage and Lois from their union. Three additional children were born in Blythe, where Walter supported the family by farming until he and Cora opened a country store. (63)

Lois met her future husband Delmar Lee Murray (b. July 27, 1908, d. April 16, 1976) while working in the Taylor family store in Blythe. Delmar was born in Altus, OK, one of eight children born to Wylie Lee and Nancy Eugenia (Jones) Murray who married on August 13, 1904, in Mangum, OK. Nancy Jones was born April 13, 1880, in Iuka, MS, and died January 21, 1931, in Frederick, OK. Her family line can be traced back to Alabama where her parents Nancy (Morton) and William Fowler Eckles Jones were born. (63)

Little is known of Delmar's father, Wylie Lee Murray, except he was born February 29, 1884, in or near Groesbeck, county seat of Limestone County, in east-central Texas and died January 19, 1944, in Bakersfield, CA. He was a migrant farmer in southeastern Oklahoma who also worked in the oil fields in Texas. He never owned his own home. Wylie's parents, James Murray and Mary Carrol (sp?) Murray were reportedly born in Texas. Oral histories state she was a full-blood Choctaw Indian. (63) Native American blood entered the Cole line through the later union of Nancy Murray and David Cole.

Delmar was raised in the town of Frederick, Tilman County, in southwest Oklahoma. He left grade school at an early age to help tend and harvest crops. He was a migrant farm worker and mechanic in the area until 1934 when he moved to Blythe in search of work during the depths of the Great Depression. The cotton sacks he carried on his journey to aid in harvesting crops in California were confiscated by authorities at the border, a practice during those years intended to protect cotton grown in California from disease and the infestation of boll weevils.

Delmar courted Lois for two years before they married. It was common then for eager couples to travel to Arizona to be married to avoid the three-day waiting period in California. Lois and Delmar attempted the trip by car, but a storm washed out the road. It was two months before they tried again and succeeded. They were married on August 12, 1938, in Yuma. They settled in a mining camp near Midland, CA, where Delmar was employed converting gypsum into wallboard. Two children, Harold Lee (b. April 5, 1939, d. November 8, 1984) and Ronald Eugene (b. September 18, 1940) were born in the hospital in nearby Blythe.

Kaiser Gypsum opened a plant in Redwood City south of San Francisco in 1941. Lois' half-brother Eddie offered Delmar a job at the facility. Delmar went ahead to find housing. Lois followed with their two sons. Nancy was born in Redwood City on November 21, 1942.

Lois' half-sister Thelma and her husband Miner Griffin moved from Blythe to Jessup Ranch outside Arroyo Grande near Pismo Beach on the central California coast in August, 1940. Their mother Cora died there on December 5, 1940, at age 56 from pneumonia contracted after washing her waist length hair on a cool day while on a vacation trip with Delmar and Lois. (63)

Delmar and the family moved from Redwood City to Arroyo Grande in 1950. Delmar worked as a carpenter at nearby Camp Cooke, later renamed Vandenberg AFB. He became the foreman of the Jessup Ranch in 1956 and the family relocated to the ranch outside Arroyo Grande. Delmar, Lois and the three children spent four years living in a ranch house heated only by fireplaces and a potbelly wood-burning kitchen stove. Lois made all of Nancy's clothes, many from flowered chicken feed sacks. It was on the ranch that Nancy learned to drive a stick shift WW II Jeep at age 13. Her chores included tending to the animals, ironing clothes at fifty cents an hour, and hand churning butter and ice cream.

The family moved back into town in 1960 when a dispute with the Jessups caused Delmar to lose the foreman position. He and other family members built a home for Lois and the children, and one next door for Lois' father Walter and his third wife Della. Walter was a renowned storyteller who remained mentally alert and active until he died June 4, 1972, at age 90 in Arroyo Grande, CA.

The children finished public school in Arroyo Grande. They picked apricots, strawberries, cherries, and beans in the summer, and Nancy ironed clothes for 50 cents an hour to earn spending money. Lois made Nancy save half of what she earned.

Nancy's brother Harold graduated from high school and drove an ambulance in the area before entering Civil Service at Vandenberg AFB. Her brother Ronald received a DVM degree from the University of California at Davis in 1964 and served in the U.S. Army before entering private practice as a veterinarian. Nancy was athletic and both a cheerleader and basketball player in high school. She graduated on June 17, 1960, and earned a certificate in business/bookkeeping from the Central California Commercial College in Fresno, CA, the next year.

Delmar and Lois moved from Arroyo Grande to Yucca Valley, CA, in 1972. Delmar died there on April 16, 1976. Lois married Donald Griffin (no relation to Miner Griffin) in 1977 and moved to Woodburn, OR. After he died in 1981, Lois returned to Arroyo Grande to be near family and friends. She died there on December 4, 1995, at age 76 from complications after a heart attack experienced while undergoing surgery to remove a nonmalignant mass from her abdomen.

Nancy found joy in music from her earliest childhood days on the ranch and by played various instruments in the school orchestra and band. She was also an accomplished singer who was called upon frequently to perform at recitals, weddings, and other events. Nancy talent led to a scholarship in music at the University of California Los Angeles. Family circumstances prevented her from accepting.

Nancy worked for the Santa Maria Times after graduating from high school in 1960 and before receiving a degree from Central California Commercial College. She was employed as a legal secretary in San Luis Obispo, as a salesperson in a dress shop in Arroyo Grande, and worked for a Ford agency in Santa Maria before entering Civil Service at Vandenberg AFB in late 1961. She was a secretary in the 1st Strategic Missile Division records management and transportation offices.

It was at a weekend party in on-base Navy Officers' Quarters in 1962 that she met David, a 1st Lieutenant in the United States Air Force assigned to the 1st Strategic Missile Division. Nancy attended the party at the insistence of her close friend Margie Luis. David and Nancy spoke only briefly, but she remarked to Margie that evening that she had just met the man she planned to marry. Imagine her disappointment when she did not hear from him for three months.

One day they met by chance in the stairway of the building where they both worked and David invited her to the Officers' Club for Friday night "happy hour". They began dating and continued to develop the relationship, even after she relocated to Downey, CA, to work for North American Aviation.

David was promoted to Captain and reassigned from Vandenberg AFB to Offutt AFB outside Omaha, NE, in January 1964. He proposed to her by phone from Omaha the following month and they were married in Lakewood, OH on May 16, 1964. David's father, Rev. Dr. Stuart G. Cole, officiated. After a brief honeymoon in Chicago on the drive to Omaha, they moved into an apartment and later bought their first home in the small community of Bellevue on the banks of the Missouri River. Within a few years she and the family moved to California, to Oklahoma, to Washington D.C., to Virginia, and back to California.

Nancy devoted her energy to raising the three sons and setting up household 23 times following Air Force reassignments and relocations throughout the United States and Europe. She remained out of the workforce to tend the family needs and, during the early years, even made many of the young boys clothes to help stretch the household budget.

While living in England in the fall of 1977, Nancy developed a severe respiratory condition and was hospitalized locally. An extremely virulent lung infection persisted for weeks and could have taken her life had she not been still young and strong. A period of bed rest followed and it was not until near Christmas that she regained her strength.

An interest in stained glass developed while she was living and studying the craft in Germany. This led eventually to the opening of her own stained-glass business after the family's return to California. Her studio was in her home in Westlake Village, CA, purchased in 1976 before moving to England and Germany, and to which they returned in 1981 after living in England and Germany. When the three sons were grown she returned to the legal profession for the first time since her marriage to David. She worked as a legal secretary for a succession of firms from 1987 to 1999, while continuing to develop her skill as a stained glass artist.

Nancy had a happy disposition and loved fresh flowers. She was an avid gardener with a natural ability to make living things flourish. She also had a facility for languages, which made her an immense help to David and the family when traveling or living overseas. She studied Spanish in school, learned German while living in Stuttgart, and turned her attention to Italian prior to an extended vacation there.

Nancy Murray Cole (1968 and 1980)

She devoted much of her spare time to the needs of St. Patrick's Episcopal Church in Thousand Oaks, serving on the Altar Guild and as its Directress. She also planted and tended gardens on the church grounds. Later she was Directress of the Altar Guild at the Church of the Epiphany in nearby Agoura before relocating to Texas with David shortly after his retirement.

She and David relocated to the Hill Country of Texas in 1999. This presented some major challenges for her gardening talents. The caliche soil in Texas has a high alkaline content. Nancy faced the test head on and became certified as a "Texas Master Gardener". She had truckloads of good soil added to the yard and garden areas surrounding the new home, selected plants that could tolerate the alkaline soil and heat of Texas summers, and learned what the resident deer population would not regularly mow to the ground. In three years her gardens received a "Backyard Wildlife Habitat Certificate" from the Texas Parks and Wildlife Department and were selected for the Fair Oaks Ranch and Boerne Garden Club annual garden tours.

In 2006 she was selected by the City of Fair Oaks Ranch to be the Director of Beautification for the community of 6,000+ citizens. As such, she worked with the city staff and various committees to landscape common areas and entrances, and advised residents with personal garden issues.

Nancy was always a quiet, gentle, sensitive person liked by all who knew her. Her house was normally adorned with freshly cut flowers. She was a caring wife, loving mother, and benevolent protector of numerous cats, always having several sharing her home and bed.

David Charles Cole

David was born at 10:30 p.m. September 22, 1936, at Syracuse Memorial Hospital in Syracuse, NY, as there was no complete-care hospital facility in the small community of Seneca Falls where his parents lived. He was baptized by his father at Trinity Episcopal Church in Seneca Falls on December 12, 1936.

The family lived in the church rectory at 90 Cayuga Street. When David was three they moved to Geneva, NY, where his father became Chaplain of Hobart and William Smith Colleges. The family lived in the rectory at 630 S. Main Street on Seneca Lake, next to the college chapel.

Five years later he moved again, this time to Rochester, NY, when his father accepted a position as Rector of the Church of the Ascension. The rectory was on a hill at 309 Maplewood Drive, several blocks from the church. The final family move occurred in the spring of 1949 when Stuart assumed a similar position at the Church of the Ascension, Lakewood, OH, west of Cleveland on the shore of Lake Erie. The rectory behind the church at 13216 Detroit Avenue served as David's home for the next 10 years.

David was a regular member of the church choir at each parish. As a result, he developed a love of classical music that stayed with him throughout his life. A sports enthusiast, he frequently asked his father's permission to skip church choir duties on warm summer mornings so he and friends could be at Cleveland's municipal stadium early to purchase $2 bleacher seats to watch the Cleveland Indians play.

At age 13, he was a candidate for attendance at St. Albans School, a college preparatory school located on the grounds of the Washington National Cathedral in Washington, DC. David's parents decided that living in a home family environment and attending the highly accredited Lakewood public high school was best for his personal development.

He was eager to work. Too young to be hired at age 14, he worked one summer as a stock boy at a small family-owned grocery store near home. He received no pay, but was allowed to choose one bag of candy from the shelf at the end of each day.

David completed high school in Lakewood and returned to Geneva in the fall of 1955 as an entering freshman at Hobart College. The fact that his father had been the college chaplain helped the admissions office overlook an unremarkable high school academic record and marginal entrance exam scores. He was allowed in, but on academic probation for the first semester.

A "late bloomer" as a student, David was a below average student in grade school, having to repeat the fifth grade, struggled in high school, but found scholastic wings in college. The fear of being sent home in disgrace was a powerful motivator. He surprised himself and his parents by achieving a 3.0 average (4.0 scale) the first two semesters, was on the dean's list in four of the eight semesters, and near the top of his graduating class.

He earned spending money while in college by working as the on-campus sales representative for the New York Times and the New York Herald Tribute (competing newspapers), as-well-as Coca-Cola and as campus representative for the Winston-Salem Tobacco Company (although he was not a smoker). He also bought, managed, and drew the profits from reconditioned cigarette machines he placed strategically in several fraternity houses. He was awarded the "Keith Lawrence Prize" given to an upperclassman "who, while earning a substantial part of his college expenses by working during the school year, has taken an active part in extra-curricular activities while maintaining an above average academic standing."

During the summers he worked from midnight until 10:00 a.m. weekdays as a stevedore for a trucking company on the docks in Cleveland. The daily tasks were physically demanding, but the pay was excellent and guaranteed he would be financially able to return to college in the fall.

David lettered in varsity lacrosse, was an honor society member, and president of Kappa Sigma fraternity. He enjoyed an active social life. William

Smith College for women is co-located with Hobart and the legal age for alcohol consumption in New York was 18 at the time.

With no particular career plans in mind, David chose psychology as his major field of study and continued his Air Force Reserve Officer Training Corps (AFROTC) studies. AFROTC participation was mandatory during the first two years at this land-grant college. Military service was required from most young men during the period. By remaining in the program in his junior and senior years, he avoided the probability of being drafted into the Army enlisted ranks upon graduation. He considered it clearly more desirable to serve the necessary three years as an officer in the Air Force instead of a private in the Army.

He was slated for pilot training after graduation from college. His Air Force Officer Qualification Test score was the highest in New York State, resulting in his being awarded the <u>Chicago Tribune</u> Silver Medal for Achievement "for his knowledge of aviation principles and display of personal characteristics such as are desirable in an officer of the United States Air Force." He was selected for entrance into flying training based on his "academic qualifications, aptitude for flying and physical fitness." It was not to be, however. While in training at MacDill AFB in Florida between his sophomore and junior year he was unable to pass a night vision test required of all pilots. He was offered navigator training, but rejected that in favor of the Public Information career field. He later considered this turn of events to be a good thing. Had he gone into pilot training he was certain he would end up in fighter jets. The Vietnam war was only a few years in the future and, had he been a jet pilot, he may not have survived to marry and enjoy a long and fruitful life.

His active military career began in August 1959 with an assignment as Special Assistant for Information, Middletown Air Material Area, Olmstead AFB, PA, near Harrisburg. His regular office number of 67971A signifying he was one of only 68,000 officers to have entered the Air Force since its establishment in 1948.

One year later David was reassigned to the American Forces Radio and Television Service (AFRTS) Korean Network (AFKN) headquarters in Seoul where he was News Director and concurrently Officer-in-Charge of the eight-station radio network. This quick succession of assignments set a pattern for his military career that ultimately included 21 relocations in 27 years, 16 of those accompanied by his wife Nancy and the children.

David became Chief of the Public Information Division, 1st Strategic Missile Division (SMD), Vandenberg AFB, CA, and aide-de-camp to the SMD vice commander in June 1961. He served there during the test/evaluation phase of the all USAF intercontinental ballistic missile (ICBM) programs, and supported USAF and NASA polar-orbiting satellite launches. He attended Squadron Officers' School in Montgomery, AL, in the spring of 1963. That fall he spent a semester in residence at the Boston University School of Communications/Public Relations, earning 12 credit hours toward an MA in Public Relations.

He nearly entered the priesthood in the Episcopal Church at this time on a Rockefeller scholarship. He had considered attending seminary for several years and had the endorsement of two bishops. However, an interview in Long Beach conducted by members of the scholarship committee squashed that idea. They were not convinced his commitment was great enough. That was probably true, as his life never skipped a beat in disappointment and he continued with the Air Force life he had come to enjoy. He was enjoying his bachelor years, driving his red Alpha Romeo Spider Veloce convertible back and forth between the base and the beaches at Santa Barbara where he spent many weekends.

The Air Force offered him a regular commission in 1963. With no other career plans and finding himself happy in both his work and Air Force life, David accepted. Along with the regular commission came an additional three-year obligation to stay in the Air Force.

He was promoted to Captain and reassigned as Chief, News Media Branch, Strategic Air Command Headquarters (SAC), at Offutt AFB near Omaha, NE, in January 1964. After arriving in Omaha in the winter, David quickly became aware of how very much he loved and missed Nancy, who had been his close friend and companion in California for more than two years.

One Saturday night in February he entered a telephone booth in a country-western bar and made the most important call of his life. Nancy said "yes" and his father conducted the wedding service in Lakewood on May 16, 1964. He was 27. She was 21. A day after the wedding, the couple headed back to Nebraska, pausing for a few days to honeymoon in Chicago before driving on to Omaha and a new life together. Between them they had $550.

David and Nancy spent four years in Nebraska living in two apartments, buying and selling a small home in Bellevue near the base, and finally renting a home in nearby Papillion. He was too junior in rank to merit housing on base. Nancy's four year old son, Christian, was adopted into the family on March 29, 1965.

The work at SAC headquarters was demanding but psychologically rewarding. He was responsible for interfacing with the news media representatives and governing the release of information on such sensitive matters as aircraft/missile accidents, nuclear deterrence policy and the control of nuclear weapons. David also supported Strategic Air Command operations in the war in Southeast Asia and in the fall of 1967 he volunteered for service in Vietnam. His orders soon came reassigning him as Chief of Media Liaison, Headquarters 7th Air Force, Tan Son Nhut AB, on the outskirts of Saigon.

As luck would have it, he submitted his volunteer statement in the late fall of 1967 before learning that Nancy was pregnant with John David, their firstborn son. Her pregnancy test had been "positive" but someone at the hospital had simply filed it away without giving them a call. Thankfully, David's departure was delayed many months and he was with Nancy for John David's birth at the Offutt AFB hospital on April 25, 1968.

Nancy and David, Christian, baby John David, and their cat Sandy piled into a compact car two weeks later and drove to Arroyo Grande, CA, where Nancy and the boys lived near her parents while David was in Southeast Asia. They drove mostly at night as it was June and the compact car had no air conditioning. It burned several valves, but made the trip to California safely.

David flew to Vietnam from the Santa Maria airport on the 4th of July weekend and moved into a "villa" in Saigon that had been modified into temporary quarters for use by public affairs officers. He and friends would sit on the rooftop patio at night with a beer in hand watching the air war being waged around the city of Saigon.

Captain David Charles Cole
Phan Rang AB, Vietnam, 1968

At nearby Tan Son Nhut Air Base he oversaw press operations and escorted members of the news media on visits to outlying bases. He was the principal point of contact on Air Force wartime activities for accredited news media representatives from around the world. He also elected to volunteer as a combat observer on AC-130 gunship and other combat missions. After several months Nancy wrote and asked why he was endangering himself by volunteering to fly missions when he had a family waiting at home. Good question! David grounded himself for the duration of the tour of duty.

Nancy and David communicated by letter nearly every day and occasionally by audiotape. On a few rare occasions they were able to talk over primitive wireless connections made possible by volunteer amateur "HAM" radio operators in the United States. The two had to speak one at a time and then say "over" so the operator could toggle a switch to allow the conversation to flow in the other direction. One night U.S. Senator Barry Goldwater (R., AZ) was the volunteer operator.

Surprise news came in the form of a call to David's office in Vietnam saying he was being promoted from Captain to Major ahead of his contemporaries—the only public affairs officer so honored. There was no official way for him to get the news to Nancy quickly, so the local CBS bureau chief offered to send her a telegram from Saigon. Nancy thought the telegram from Vietnam meant David been injured or killed. She sat with the missive in her lap for a long time before gathering the courage to open it. When she did, her fears turned into double joy.

David returned to California on July 4, 1969, to rejoin Nancy and the two boys. They were soon in the car again and off to Norman, OK, where he earned an MA in Journalism/Public Relations from the University of Oklahoma. David completed his masters course work and thesis within 10 months while maintaining a 4.0 average, a feat he admitted he could not have accomplished without Nancy's help. She watched over the boys and typed all his papers and thesis flawlessly before the days of word processors.

In May 1970 they were back in the car enroute to an assignment with the Public Information Division in the Office of the Secretary of the Air Force in the Pentagon. The family lived in Arlington, VA, for 30 months, first renting a home at 6022 North 9th Road and then at 864 Longfellow Drive. The last of their three sons, Carter, was born at Walter Reed Medical Center on June 26, 1971.

In January 1973 the family moved again, this time to the Norfolk Naval Base where David became a student at the Armed Forces Staff College. Following graduation in June, they drove back to the West Coast where he became Deputy Chief of the Secretary of the Air Force Office of Information in Los Angeles supporting the Secretary during his travels throughout the western United States. Secretary of the Air Force Thomas Reid sent David a personal letter of thanks for his help, noting: "The United States Air Force is fortunate to talent such as yours working in its behalf." A promotion to Lt. Colonel soon followed.

David and Nancy borrowed against two small life insurance policies, secured a VA loan and purchased a home at 10003 Encino Avenue in Northridge. The property was a "fixer". The young couple worked hard making improvements to the structure, yard, and oversized pool. David earned a Real Estate license and worked as a salesman on weekends to supplement his Air Force income. Finances were tight, but family life was close-knit and special.

Their home was located in the heart of the San Fernando Valley. They lived there until the summer of 1976 when a growing family and concern about earthquakes caused them to leave "the Valley" to a newer home at 3166 W. Black Hills Court in Westlake Village. A major earthquake struck the Valley in 1991, severely damaging the home they had sold in Northridge.

Less than a year after moving into their new home, David received a telephone call at the office offering him an assignment as part of the Royal Air Force Exchange Program in England. He had found success working as real estate agent on weekends and considered turning down the assignment and retiring from the Air Force to continue his civilian career. Nancy had never traveled overseas and wanted the opportunity to live in Europe. He elected to accept the assignment.

They rented their new home to a young family, shipped the Volkswagen Beatle "bug" to England, and flew off to London in June 1977. After an orientation visit there, David entered the Royal Air Force senior professional college at RAF Cranwell, near the village of Sleaford in Lincolnshire. The air college at RAF Cranwell is the oldest such institution in the world. He was the first public affairs officer and only non-flying USAF officer ever selected to study at the college. As one of the few "colonial" families in the area, the family lived among and like their Royal Air Force counterparts. The two youngest boys attended local schools and Christian was a boarding student at the Air Force High School at RAF High Wycombe outside London.

The red brick on-base RAF quarters assigned to the family was wonderfully cool in the summer but drafty in winter, with no central heating. Family members would all run from the parlor with its electric fireplace up the stairs to separate bedrooms each night as blowing snow piled inside on the windowsills.

As part of the #34 Air Warfare Course student body, David was expected to join the cricket team and compete against the faculty/staff and enter the class squash competition. The student team beat the staff and David won the class squash tournament. To the amusement of his classmates he suffered a nasty broken nose in the process when surprised by a sweeping backhand of a left-handed female player.

It was a pleasant life. The family was treated well by their Royal College hosts and the families of the select group of course participants (one Ministry of Defence (sic) officer, thirteen RAF officers, one Royal Navy pilot, plus one pilot each from Canada, Australia, and New Zealand). Air Force types from every nation are affable and the assignment committed David and Nancy to a full social schedule with their course counterparts, both in their quarters and at the Officers' Mess. Sunday service at the on-base chapel, where both sang in the choir, was often followed by sherry at Mess while the boys played croquet on the lawn. His critique from the commandant at course end noted: "David and his wife contributed very fully to the social life of the course and were extremely hospitable and charming hosts, and undoubtedly a most popular couple."

Commenting on Lt. Colonel Cole's participation in the course, deputy commandant, Air Commodore Carver wrote: " . . . he stood out as an extremely keen and capable student, totally involved in all aspects of the course and willing and able to make a massive contribution from his own specialized knowledge . . . I am grateful to have been sent an Information Officer of such quality to undertake the Royal Air Force's most senior professional course."

After completing his course work in early December 1977, David was reassigned as Chief, Plans and Programs Division and soon Deputy Director, Office of Public Affairs, United States European Command (EUCOM) at Patch Barracks near Vaihingen on the outskirts of Stuttgart, Germany. EUCOM was the senior military headquarters for all U.S. forces in Europe.

A lack of immediately available on-base housing meant Nancy and the boys had to remain behind in England for the remainder of the winter of 1977-1978. They did not rejoin him until a two-bedroom apartment was secured months later in the German village of Magstadt outside Stuttgart. David flew back to England and the family made the move to Germany in the family Volkswagen: four of them, Sandy the cat, and the plants inside with their belongings on a roof rack. Within a few months, the family was able to move into three-bedroom officers' quarters on Patch Barracks.

David was promoted to Colonel in the fall of 1979 after only 20 years of service. He pinned on his new "eagles" ahead of schedule (in Air Force terms, he was "frocked") under a special directive issued by Air Force Personnel Center in Texas at the request of the EUCOM Commander.

He was in Stockholm on business in January 1980 when the phone rang in his hotel room. A voice from the Pentagon told him he was to be immediately reassigned to serve as the Director of Public Affairs for United States Air Force in Europe (USAFE) and, simultaneously, Public Information Officer for NATO's Allied Air Forces Central Europe. The Commander-in-Chief of USAFE had just fired the colonel who had held those positions.

Both commands were headquartered at Ramstein Air Base near Kaiserslautern, a two-hour drive from Stuttgart. David flew home, packed his bags, kissed Nancy, and moved into the visiting officers' quarters at Ramstein. Nancy and the boys remained behind at Patch Barracks for several months until on-base housing could be arranged at the new location.

In his new capacity he directed the largest public affairs program in the Air Force supervising more than 500 public affairs and broadcast personnel at 37 locations in 11 countries stretching from England to Turkey. But, there was always time for the family. Sundays were often spent hiking ("Volksmarching") through German woods and villages, usually followed by wurst, sauerkraut and, for Nancy and David, a stein or two of the local *biers*. The years in Germany were exciting and the family was able to travel widely from the Netherlands to Italy.

The Air Force Public Affairs career field had only two general officer positions—both in the Pentagon in Washington. Three and four-star general officer endorsement of his annual efficiency reports consistently recommended him for immediate advancement to the rank of brigadier general. David and Nancy discussed their options before leaving Germany. For the welfare of the children and with concern about the stress related to another assignment in the Pentagon, David took his name out of contention by rejecting an opportunity to return to the Office of the Secretary of the Air Force in Washington. He never regretted the decision.

The family was therefore able to return to their home in Westlake Village in July 1981 when David accepted an offer from the Department of Defense to fulfill duties as Commander, Armed Forces Radio and Television Broadcast Center (AFRTS-BC) in Hollywood serving 1.2 million service members and their families around the world. It was the only command position open to public affairs officers, who normally serve as a member of a commander's staff. He was responsible for meeting the radio and television news/information/entertainment needs of armed forces radio and television stations at more than 600 locations around the globe—providing professional, contemporary programming to the largest radio/TV network in the world at the time. His annual budget was in excess of $23 million.

David remained active in the local government and church affairs in Westlake Village, served as homeowner association president for seven years, and as Senior Warden at the local Episcopal parish. When the boys left for college, Nancy returned to her stained glass work in earnest and directed the activities of the Altar Guild at the family's parish.

He spent five years at AFRTS-BC during which time David directed the construction of a totally new broadcast center, greatly expanded network direct satellite programming, and raised overseas prime-time program material to 92% of that available to viewers in the United States. In the summer of 1986 he was offered command of the Pacific Stars and Stripes newspaper headquarted in Tokyo, Japan, but declined, as a family move would have been a hardship on his sons, one about to enter college, one in high school, and one working in the area.

David retired from the Air Force in December 1986 at age 50. Among his 18 medals and military decorations were the Defense Distinguished Service

Medal, Legion of Merit, Bronze Star, USAF Meritorious Service Medal, and Vietnam Service Ribbon with five battle stars. The Government of the Republic of Vietnam awarded him the Air Service Medal for his actions during the war.

Upon the event of David's retirement, the Chief of Staff of the Air Force wrote:

> *Dear Dave:*
> *I've followed your progress closely and must say you've accomplished more than I thought possible. There are thousands of service men and women and their families who have benefited—and will continue to benefit—from your initiative and leadership as Commander of AFRTS.*
> *Thanks, Dave, and best wishes as you begin a new career later this year.*
> *CHARLES A. GABRIEL, General, USAF, Chief of Staff.*

David accepted a position as President of CBX Systems, Inc., an electronics design firm located in Burbank. He resigned after nine months, however, when it became clear the company could not prosper during the economic recession gripping the industry and upon learning his business partner was professionally unprincipled when dealing with government contracts. Time in prison was not in David's plans!

In February 1988 he began a second career when he became the Director of Public Affairs for The Aerospace Corporation, a private, nonprofit company engaged in the design/engineering of launch vehicles and satellite systems for the USAF Space and Missile Systems Center in El Segundo, near the Los Angeles International Airport. Here he returned to the space business he supported at Vandenberg AFB 25 years earlier. The company was the principal supplier of engineering support for USAF, NASA and National Security Agency satellite systems.

David received the corporation's President's Award for Administrative Achievement two years later and was promoted to be the Principal Director of a newly created Corporate Communications Directorate where he led a staff of 160 employees responsible for all employee and external information activities. He was a member of the Public Relations Society of America, Society of Professional Journalists, and Aviation/Space Writers' Association. He retired from The Aerospace Corporation in August 31, 1999, at age 63 after completing an 11-year civilian career in the aerospace industry and 40 years to the month after initially entering active duty status in the Air Force in 1959. Nancy said "goodbye" to her friends in the legal offices of Morrow et al. the same month after 10 years with the firm.

One motivation for retiring was the daily commute from Westlake Village to the Aerospace complex near the Los Angeles International airport. The

96-mile roundtrip by car added more than two hours to every business day. In his 11 years with the company, David commuted in excess of 250,000 accident free miles (equal to 89 roundtrips between LA and New York) and spent more than 5,500 hours (equal to 230 24-hour days) behind the wheel.

The Aerospace President/CEO, Edward C. Aldridge Jr., former Secretary of the Air Force and NASA astronaut, wrote: "Thank you for your support to me during your tour . . . you and your staff were a valuable part of the corporation".

David and Nancy sold their Westlake Village home and moved into an apartment in Austin, TX, in October 1999. This allowed them to visit Fair Oaks Ranch in the Texas Hill Country 30 miles north of San Antonio as necessary to watch over the final construction phases of their new home. It also provided an opportunity to spend many pleasant hours with their son John David and his fiancée Amy who lived in the same Austin apartment complex.

They were honored before leaving Westlake Village when their home was chosen as one of the five most attractive in the area and was part of the annual garden tour held to fund college scholarships. More than 700 garden enthusiasts visited to study plants, trees, and landscaping ideas Nancy had incorporated during the 23 years they owned the home.

One of Nancy's biggest stained glass projects was designing, selecting materials for, and supervising the creation and installation of a five-foot diameter circular window installed over the main entrance to the Church of the Epiphany, their local Episcopal parish. The window was dedicated to deceased members of the Murray and Cole families on September 19, 1999, two weeks before the move to Texas.

Nancy's glass inventory was too precious to trust to a commercial mover. So, David loaded the glass and many of their possessions in a 28' Ryder truck and drove to Austin. Nancy and the cats followed closely in the family car.

They stored many items in Austin while living in the apartment. Later, they rented another truck and took the items to Fair Oaks Ranch. While unloading some of them into the new home, David fell backwards from the bed of the truck to the concrete driveway six feet below. Thankfully, nothing was hurt except his pride. David and Nancy moved in on November 12, 1999. Christian and his young son Alex came a few weeks later with a second 28' truck from California containing the remainder of the household goods.

Their new home on the golf course at 30322 Fairway Run Drive in Fair Oaks Ranch was completed on schedule. It was custom designed to meet their needs in retirement and included a studio where Nancy could continue to create her stained glass artwork under the business name "Patterns in Glass".

Though ebullient by nature, David experienced a sudden onset of clinical depression a few months after settling into the new home. It seemed to surface within a day or two and his dark moods took hold frequently over a number of weeks. It could not be explained by anything in his life, which, at that stage, was nearly stress free. He discussed it with Nancy and then sought professional help. The psychiatrist explained the bouts were brought on by a temporary chemical imbalance in his brain and resulted from a hereditary predisposition. His grandfather on his mother's side of the family, his mother, and his brother had all suffered sometimes debilitating depression. The onset occurred at various states in each of their lives. In David's case, he was 64 before any signs surfaced. His recent retirement and the accompanying abrupt end of a professional life filled with heavy responsibilities may have served as a trigger. A daily mild dose of the anti-depressant Effexor corrected the condition within a very few days. The symptoms did not return.

David eased into retirement by leading Bible study groups; volunteering to be an associate coach of lacrosse at St. Mary's Hall prep school; tutoring abused and abandoned children at Father Flanagan's Girls and Boys Town shelter in San Antonio; serving as Chairman of its Board; and giving his time as vice chair of the San Antonio American Red Cross Armed Forces Emergency Services Board. Twice he traveled to Peidras Negras, Mexico, with church construction teams to help build homes for the less fortunate.

He also started a business importing and wholesaling various products throughout Texas. The sole proprietorship was registered under the name DANCO (short for David and Nancy Cole) and helped fund frequent vacations and cruises to the warm waters of the Pacific and Caribbean where the two found great joy in scuba diving and snorkeling.

His was a life well traveled. Beginning in 1960 he lived, sojourned or vacationed in Korea, Japan, the Philippines, Thailand, Vietnam, Singapore, Hong Kong, Iceland, England, Germany, Spain, Denmark, Norway, Sweden, Austria, Italy, Turkey, Israel, Greece, Mexico, Tahiti, Malaysia, Canada, and numerous Caribbean islands, and holidayed frequently in each of the Hawaiian Islands.

David's years in the Air Force fostered a desire to stay physically fit. He played tennis and squash well into his 40s, ran a mile or two every day into his 60s, and then relied on coaching duties and aerobic machines at local health clubs to stay in shape. In 2003, after two years with the lacrosse program at St. Mary's Hall (SMH) prep school in San Antonio, he accepted a position as head lacrosse coach at a local Episcopal prep school, the Texas Military Institute (TMI). Lacrosse was a new sport at TMI. David built the program from scratch. He racked up two winning seasons as head coach there before moving on to help another struggling high school team. In his years at SMH and TMI his teams won 75% of their contests, recording 36 wins against only 12 losses.

"Coach Cole" found great satisfaction in working with young people and continued to teach the game past age 70. He returned to the Hobart College campus for four years to coach at summer youth lacrosse camps there. The college newsletter reported: "He commands the field with the ease and grace of a man used to achieving results. He moves among (the players) with competence, calling out suggestions while complimenting success, and has the full attention of every boy on the field." An assembly of coaches and players honored David in 2005 on his last day at camp. The College president, Mark D. Gearan, who had been Deputy Chief of Staff in the Clinton White House and Director of the US Peace Corps, led the ceremony.

His service record entitled him to burial with full military honors at Arlington National Military Cemetery. Instead, both he and Nancy directed that, upon their deaths, their ashes were to be spread in the sea on the far side of Molokini crater, a volcanic outcropping off the southwest coast of Maui. David and Nancy had:

Christian Marlon Cole, b. June 28 1960, Oakland, CA. child of Nancy Murray, adopted March 29, 1965, Bellevue, NE.
John David Cole, b. April 25, 1968, USAF Hospital, Offutt AFB, NE.
Carter Nicholas Cole, b. June 26, 1971, USA Walter Reed Medical Center, Washington, DC

The 12th Generation in 1987 (from upper right)
Carter Nicholas Cole, John David Cole and Christian Marlon Cole

Summary Comments

"In the annals of this country, the (Daniel) Cole family is old. It has been seen and participated in everything of moment from Puritan days to the present time. In the records of great achievements, it is not particularly noted, but, as a race, the Coles have proved themselves sturdy, courageous, self-reliant and independent." (19, p. 4)

Several things can be written with certainty about this branch of the Cole family. They were solid citizens: merchants, farmers, laborers, clergymen and, starting in the ninth generation, business and military professionals. They were God loving, compassionate and unselfish, giving freely of their energy for family, church, community, and country. They were hearty, industrious, law-abiding, congenial, and faithful to their marriages, separating only in death. They also were patriots who defended their beliefs, being involved in some capacity in The Revolutionary War, War of 1812, Civil War, World War I, World War II, and Vietnam War.

They came primarily from English yeoman stock. While not aristocratic, they are all descendants of a Pilgrim settler and signer of the Mayflower Compact. (79) German bloodlines were mixed with the English in the ninth generation; Irish, Scottish, and Canadian in the tenth; and American Indian in the eleventh.

Members of this branch of the Daniel Cole family in America have lived long lives, with males in the line averaging 72 years and their female partners 70 years, calculated from dates that are known. This is quite remarkable, given the shorter life-spans common in the 17th, 18th, and 19th centuries. There is no evidence of significant genetic deficiencies or chronic ailments, other than a tendency toward mild depression and a potential for alcoholism introduced by the distaff side of the family in the 10th generation. There is a natural disposition to male (42) instead of female (24) progeny. Only one set of twins appears in the line.

Our early ancestors received very little formal education. Higher levels of education did not become the norm until the ninth generation when Frank and Rose Cole put three of their four children through college. Later generations have been college graduates and more prosperous.

As in all families, fate has played a decisive role. Had the minie ball that entered the right side of yet unmarried Charles Lewis Cole been fatal, or the two Southern women and Negro man not nursed him back to life, this branch of the Cole family would have ended in a North Carolina field on March 8, 1865.

A genealogical trail has no end—only stopping places. As I switch off the computer for the final time I trust members of the family will read this document with interest, develop an understanding and appreciation for their ancestry, and record contemporary details to extend the story to benefit future generations.

I take comfort in knowing that when future members of the family read these words, part of me will be there also. The only immortality one can hope for is found in contemplation by others.

1897

1620

This certifies that _____ STEPHEN HOPKINS _____ _Mayflower Ancestor_

_____ DAVID CHARLES COLE _____ is a member of

the General Society of Mayflower Descendants founded 12 January, 1897,

to perpetuate the memory of the Pilgrims, to maintain and defend the prin-

ciples of civil and religious liberty, to cherish and maintain the ideals and

institutions of American Freedom and to oppose any theories or actions that

threaten their continuity.

Richard Haldane Brownell Governor General

Caroline Lewis Kendall Historian General

Signing of the Mayflower Compact, 21 November, 1620

Mayflower Society House — Plymouth, Massachusetts

Anno Domini

September 27, 1997

CALIFORNIA _____ Society No. 6421 _____ General No. 64103

Area Map of Eastham, Cape Cod, 1998
(Cole Road Marks Area of Original Cole Farm)

Index of Illustrations

Index of Family Names

One of the inevitable consequences of covering 370 years of family history in a single volume is that little can be researched on early members and sometimes too many details are available concerning the lives of the later members. The result is an inverted pyramid of useable information. The author is sensitive to the fact this work includes more information on his life than on his progenitors, but hopes those who follow in the line will understand and record their life events in similar detail to benefit future generations.

The following index contains names found in this work beginning with page 13. Authors or titles of works referenced in the text are excluded. Given names of male progenitors in the family line from are shown in bold face. Baptismal names are provided, when know, and listed without parentheses. Maiden names are shown in parenthesis under the new family name, and these females are also listed under their original family name.

Rebecca (_____) 40
Ruth (Cole, Young) 40
BELL
Elizabeth 93
BERRY
Jabez 47
Rebecca 47
Susan 48, 49
BISHOP
Alice 28
BOETIKER
Anna 75
BOND
Hannah 43
Mary 43
BOUTON
Elizabeth 49
BOWEN
Amy Kass 108
Elizabeth 41
BRADFORD
William 23, 25
BREWSTER
Love 15
William 15, 21, 93
BROWN
Joseph 39
Martha 39
BUDD
Fannie Ames 68
Frank Ames 68
John Spafford 68
Sarah (Ames) 68
BUEHLER
Friedrich 70
BURPEE
Evelyn Woodbury 91
CHANDLER/CHAUNDELER/
CHANDELER
Edmond 34, 35
Elizabeth 34

Jane (Gitton) 34
John 34
Ruth 34, 35
CHASE
Alvin 49
Obediah 48, 49
Ruth (Cole) 49
Susan (Berry) 49
CHESTER
Dorothy (Hooker) 35
John 35
Mary (_____) 35
Ruth 35
CHILDS
Hannah 40
CHIPMAN
John 28
CLARK
Jane 14
CLARKE
Martha 28
COLE:
Abner 42
Alex 108
Amy Kass (Bowen) 108
Amy Woodbury 92
Anna (Hermann) 78
Anna 49
Anne (_____) 31, 36, 43
Ariel 42
Asahel 49, 52, 53, 58
Berry 48
Carter Nicholas 103, 110, 111
Catherine Irene 78
Charity (Hazen) 46
Charity 42
Charles Frederick 77, 79, 91
Charles Green 49, 50, 52-55, 59
Charles Lewis 36, 56, 57, 59-68,
    77, 80, 114
Christian Marlon 101, 102, 104,
    108, 110, 111

NICHOLS
    Elizabeth (Bouton) 48
    Henry 48
    Josiah 48
NIKERSON
    Mercy 16
    Robert 16
OGDEN
    Mary 47
    Susan 49
PAINE
    Mary 20, 34
PATCHEN
    George 52
    Phebe (Rockwell) 52
    Uriah 52
PIERCE
    Silas 43
REED
    Sec. A.F. Thomas C.
RING
    Elizabeth 42
ROGERS
    Abigail 40
    James 40
    Joseph 25
    Mary 40
    Mary (Paine) 20, 34, 40
    Mary (Snow) 40
    Samuel (aka James) 40
SAVORY
    Ira 52
    Lavinia (Richardson) 52
    Mary Ann 52
SMALLEY/SMALE/SMALEE/SMALLY
    Hannah (Gross) 43
    Hannah 31
    Jane 43
    Jane (Cole, Gross) 43, 44
    John, 25, 28
    Joseph 43, 44

    Mercy (Young) 44
    Priscilla 31, 43, 44
    Priscilla (Young) 44
    Samuel 43
SMITH
    Charles G. 47
    Jesse 47
    Capt. John 20
    Margaret (Cole) 47
    Thomas 40
SNOW:
    Constance (Hopkins) 19, 20, 36, 39, 40
    Hannah 20, 30, 31, 36, 42, 44
    Joseph 40
    Mark 26, 28
    Mary 20, 40
    Nicholas 20, 25, 26, 28, 36, 39, 40
    Ruth 20, 39
    Stephen 20, 36, 40, 42
    Susanna (Dean-Rogers) 20, 42
SOUTHWORTH
    Constant 28
SPIETH
    Rosina Katharina 70
STEWART
    Henry 59
    Hepsibah (Van Loom) 59
    Mary Almira 59
TAYLOR:
    Christopher Columbus 93
    Cora Elma (Baker, Hayes) 93-95
    Della (Rouse) 95
    Eliza (_____) 93
    Elizabeth (Bell) 93
    Lois Evelyn 93-95
    Col. Richard 93
    Walter Ethmer 93-95
    Pres. Zachary 93

Special thanks to Nancy Murray Cole for her help in assembling this index of names

Bibliography

1. American Genealogist, The, Vol. 42; pages 119-121, 1966, and Vol. 49, pages 215-216, 1973 (Library of Congress)

2. Anderson, Robert Charles. The Great Migration Begins—Immigrants to New England 1620-1633, Vol. I A-F; New England Historic Genealogical Society, Boston 1995 (New England Historic Genealogical Society)

3. Arber, Edward. The Story of the Pilgrim Fathers—1606-1623; Ward and Downey Ltd., London, 1897 (Boston Public Library)

4. Arden, Juliette. Cole: 200-1920 A.D., Tercentenary Edition; Lent & Graff, New York, 1920 (LA Public Library)

5. Austin, John D. Mayflower Families Through Five Generations Vol. 6—Steven Hopkins; (Third Edition) General Society of Mayflower Descendants, Boston, 2001 (New England Historic Genealogical Society)

6. Banks, Charles Edward. Planters of the Commonwealth, 1620-1640; Genealogical Publishing Co., Baltimore, 1967 (Library of Congress)

7. Banks, Charles Edward. Topographical Director of 2885 English Emigrants to New England, 1620-1650; Southern Book Company, Baltimore, 1957 (Library of Congress).

8. Banks, Charles Edward. Winthrop Fleet of 1630; Genealogical Publishing Company, Boston, 1968 (Library of Congress)

9. Bradford, William. History of Plymouth Plantation—1620-1647; The Massachusetts Historical Society, Boston 1912 (Boston Public Library)

10. Briggs, Eva Grace Fraser. Genealogy of the Coles and Allied Families; personal typed manuscript, 1928 (Library of Congress) (Not Recommended. Oral history that conflicts with documented facts in other publications).

11. Byrne, Thomas E. Chemung County, New York, History—1890-1975, Chemung Historical Society, Inc., Elmira, NY (personal copy)

12. Byrne, Thomas E. "Elmira's Civil War Prison Camp: 1864-65", The Chemung Historical Journal, Vol. 10, No. 1; September, 1964, pp. 1279-1293, Chemung Historical Society, Inc., Elmira, NY (personal copy)

13. Coldham, Peter Wilson. The Complete Book of Emigrants—1607-1660 Genealogical Publishing Co., Inc. Baltimore, 1987. (Library of Congress)

14. Cole, Ernest Byron. Descendants of James Cole of Plymouth, 1663; Grafton Press, New York, 1908 (Library of Congress)

15. Cole, Frank T. Early Genealogies of the Cole Families in America; Hann & Adair, Columbus, OH, 1887 (LA Public Library)

16. Cole, James Edwin. Genealogy of the Family of Cole, of the County of Devon; James Russell Smith Publisher, London, 1867 (Library of Congress)

17. Colker, Meredith B., Jr. Founders of Early American Families—Emigrants from Europe 1607-1657; Founders and Patriots of America, Cleveland, OH, 1985 (LA Public Library)

18. Cooper, Agnes Thomson and John Bradley. Beginnings—Thomas Cooper of Springfield and Some Allied Families; Gateway Press, Inc., Baltimore, 1987 (LA Public Library)

19. Curtis, Joseph O. Descendants of Elisha Cole; T.A. Wright, New York, 1909 (personal copy)

20. Deyo, Simeon L., edited by. History of Barnstable County Massachusetts; H. W. Blake & Co., New York 1890 (Boston Public Library)

21. Freeman, Frederick, and Rand, Geo., C. and Cornhill, Avery. The History of Cape Cod—Annals of the Thirteen Towns of Barnstable County, Vol. II; Boston, 1862 (Boston Public Library)

22. Germans to America—Lists of Passengers Arriving at U.S. Ports, 1850-1897; Vols. 14 and 16, ed. Ira Glazier/William Filby, Scholarly Resources, Inc., Wilmington, Del., 1991 (Library of Congress)

23. Hills, Leon Clark. Cape Cod Series, Vol. 1, History and Genealogy of the Planters and First Comers to Ye Old Colonie; Genealogical Publishing Company Baltimore, 1936 (Daniel Cole Society)

24. History of AFRTS—"The First 500 Years"; Department of Defense, Government Printing Office, Washington, D.C., 1992

25. History of Tioga, Chemung, Tompkins, and Schuyler Counties; Everts & Ensign, Philadelphia, 1879 (Chemung County Historical Society)

26. Hoar, Victor M. "Civil War Centennial: Sketches of Elmira's 107th Infantry Regiment", The Chemung Historical Journal, March 1960. pp. 677-681, Chemung Historical Society Inc., Elmira, NY (personal copy)

27. Holmes, Clayton Wood. The Elmira Prison Camp: A History of the Military Prison at Elmira, NY, July 6, 1864, to July, 10, 1865; G.P. Putnam's Sons, New York, 1911 (University of California Santa Barbara Library)

28. Ingham, John N. Biographical Dictionary of American Business Leaders; Greenwood Press, Westport, CT, 1983 (UCLA Research Library)

29. Kingsbury, Anna C. and Nickerson, William E. A Historical Sketch of William Collier; private printing, 1925 (DAR Library, Washington)

30. Kittredge, Henry C. Cape Cod—Its People and Their History; Houghton Mifflin Company, Boston and New York, 1930 (Boston Public Library)

31. Lancour, Harold, Compiled by and Wolfe, Richard J., (revised/enlarged Third Edition) Bibliography of Ship Passenger Lists, 1538-1825; New York Public Library

32. Lowe, Alice A. Nauset on Cape Cod, A History of Eastham; Eastham Historical Society. Shank Printer Printing, Provincetown, Massachusetts, 1968 (personal copy)

33. Lowell, Mary Chandler. Edmond Chaundeler, Geoffrey Parsons and AlliedFamilies, T.R. Marum & Sons, Boston, 1911 (New England Historic Genealogical Society)

34. Luik, Ernst. Heimatbuch (Book of the Homeland), Oberhof—Kimmichweiler Geschichte und Geshichten (History and Stories); private, 1996 (personal copy)

35. Morton, Nathaniel. New England's Memorial; Congregational Board of Publication, Boston, 1855 (Boston Public Library)

36. Murphy, Jim. The Boys' War: Confederate and Union Soldiers Talk About the War; Clarion Books, Houghton Miffin Co., Boston, 1990 (Frank W. Cole, personal copy)

37. Murray, Marian. From Rome to Ringling-Circus; Appleton-Century-Crofts, Inc., New York, 1956 (UCLA Research Library)

38. Neff, Lewis Edwin, revised by. Mayflower Index, Vol. 1-2; The General Society of Mayflower Descendants, Boston, 1960 (Library of Congress)

39. Paine, Gustave Swift. Daniel Cole and Ruth Chester: Notes on Some of Their Descendants; typed, New York, 1946 (Library of Congress)

40. Pelletrean, William S. History of Putnam County; W. W. Preston & Co., Philadelphia, 1886 (Decendants of Daniel Cole Society)

41. Pilgrim Genealogy, History and Biography; The Mayflower Descendant, Vol. V; Boston, Massachusetts Society of Mayflower Descendants, 1903 (Library of Congress)

42. Pope, Charles Henry. Pioneers of Massachusetts; Genealogical Publishing Company, Baltimore, 1969 (Library of Congress)

43. Putnam, Eden, Communicated by. Two Early Passenger Lists, 1635-1637; Reprinted from The New England Historical and Genealogical Register for July 1921, Genealogical Publishing Company, Baltimore, 1964 (Library of Congress)

44. Savage, James, Genealogical Dictionary of the First Settlers of New England—BeforeMay, 1692, Vol. I; Genealogical Publishing Company, Baltimore, 1986 (Boston Public Library)

45. Seavy, Linda L. "Focus on Newark: The Motor City of Wayne County", The Drumlins Magazine of Wayne County, Vol. 1 No. 2; January/February, 1994 (personal copy)

46. Shaw, Hubert Kinney. Families of Pilgrims; Massachusetts Society of Mayflower Descendants, Boston, 1956 (National Archives)

47. Sherman, Robert M. Mayflower Families Through Five Generations Vol. 2 —Families of James Chilton, Richard More, Thomas Rogers; General Society of Mayflower Descendants, Boston, 1995 (New England Historic Genealogical Society)

48. Sherman, Robert M. Mayflower Families Through Five Generations Vol. 15—Families of James Chilton & Richard More; General Society of Mayflower Descendants, Boston, 1997 (New England Historic Genealogical Society)

49. Shuffelton, Frank "Thomas Hooker, 1586-1647", Princeton University Press, Princeton, NJ 1977 (New York Public Library)

50. Shurtleff, Nathaniel B., edited by. Records of the Colony of New Plymouth, Miscellaneous Records 1633-1689; William White Press, Boston, 1857 (Library of Congress)

51. Smith, Patricia Ruth. Dusk to Dawn: An American Ancestry of Andrew Cole and Acenith Bishop; Royell Pub. Ltd., Alberta, Canada, 1977 (Library of Congress)

52. Stoddard, Francis R. The Truth About the Pilgrims; Society of Mayflower Descendants, New York, 1952 (Boston Public Library)

53. Stratton, Eugene Aubrey. Plymouth Colony-Its History and People, 1620-1691; Ancestry Publishing, Salt Lake City, 1986 (Library of Congress)

54. Taylor, Eva. A Short History of Elmira; Elmira, NY, 1937 (Steele Memorial Library, Elmira)

55. Tepper, Michael. American Passenger Arrival Records; Genealogical Publishing Company, Baltimore, 1988 (Library of Congress).

56. Watous, Hilda R. The County Between the Lakes; Heart of the Lakes, 1988 (DAR Library, Washington, D.C.)

57. Weller, Edwin. A Civil War Courtship: The Letters of Edwin Weller From Antietamto Atlanta. Edited by William Walton, Garden City, NY; Doubleday, 1980. (personal copy)

58. Willison, George F. Saints and Strangers; Time-Life Books, Alexandria, Virginia, 1954 (Library of Congress)

59. Winsor, Justin. History of the Town of Duxbury Massachusetts with Genealogical Registers; Crosby & Nichols, Boston, 1849 (Boston Public Library)

60. Woodworth-Barnes, Esther Littleford. Mayflower Families Through Five Generations Vol. 16, Part I—Family of John Alden; General Society of Mayflower Descendants, Boston, 1999 (New England Historic Genealogical Society)

BIBILIOGRAPHY ADDENDUM

61. Personal Recollections and Family Records, Doris (Lyons) Rothe and Donald Lyons c/o 16 Musket Trail, Simsbury, CN. 06070

62. Personal Recollections and Family Records, Frank H. Cole, Center Street, Box 2, Bemus Point, NY 14712

63. Personal Recollections and Family Records. Lois (Taylor-Murray) Griffin, 341 Beta Court, Arroyo Grande, CA. 93420 (Deceased)

64. Personal Recollections and Family Records. Stuart H. Cole, 5286 Via Murcia, Yorba Linda, CA. 92686 (Deceased)

65. Personal Recollections and Family Records of the author. David C. Cole, 30322 Fairway Run Drive, Fair Oaks Ranch, TX 78015 (830-755-4608)

66. Family Records. Rosemarie (Cole) Martineau, Rt. #3, Box 115, Morrisville, NY 13408 (315/684-3778)

67. Family Records. Patricia (Cole-Colegrove-Ballard) Jones, 2010 Tracy Street, Endwell, NY 13760

68. Family Records. Mrs. Nancy Lee Graham, 2 Parker Circle, Elmira, NY 14901 (607/732-4127)

69. Family Records. Dr. Nona Grotecloss, P.O. Box 1661, Dade City, FL 33526-1661 (Deceased)

70. Mr. and Mrs. Gregory (Debbie and Greg) Starner, 61 Beaver Dams Rd., Beaver Dams, NY 14812 (July, 2002)

71. Family Records. Architect Albert Kimmich, Ringelweg 19, 7300 Esslingen, Germany. (Phone: 07 11/31 1348)

72. Records. City of Esslingen am Neckar, Marketplatz 20, Württemberg, Germany.

73. Records. Schuyler County Historical Society, 108 N. Catherine Street, Montour Falls, NY 14865 (607/535-9741)

74. Records (as reported and sourced in the newsletter). Descendants of Daniel Cole Society; P.O. Box 367, Mahopoc Falls, NY 10542

75. Records. Wayne County Historical Society, 21 Butternut Street, Lyons, NY 14489 (315/946-4943)

76. Records. Beaver Dams United Methodist Church, courtesy of Mr. Carl W. Elder, 2222 Hornby Road, Beaver Dams, NY 14812

77. Deeds and Plat Maps. Town of Catlin, dated 1863. (personal copies)

78. The Church of Jesus Christ of Latter-Day Saints, International Genealogical Index (Library of Congress)

79. The General Society of Mayflower Descendants, Plymouth, MA (General No. 645103)

80. Family Trees, Ancestry Word Tree Project: Mason-Hyde, <marvbanker@msn. com Ancestry.com.> 2004

81. New York in the Revolution, Vol. 1, New York State Archives, Albany, NY